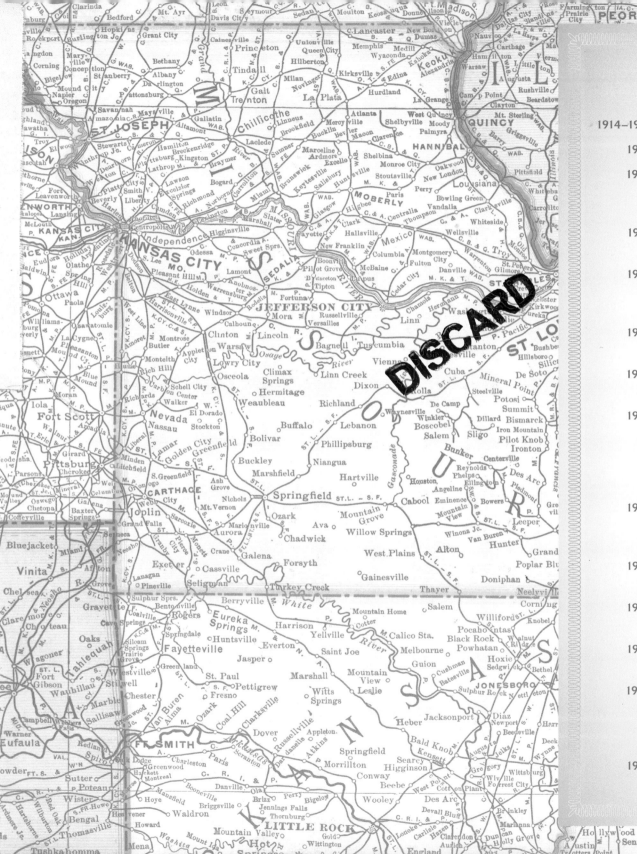

TIME LINE

1914–1918	World War I.
1929	Great Depression begins.
1930	Massive unemployment spreads across the country. Farmers begin to lose their land in bank foreclosures.
1931	Severe drought strikes the Great Plains. Dust storms begin.
1932	Dust storms increase in ferocity and number, with fourteen major storms in this year alone. Franklin D. Roosevelt elected president.
1933	Thirty-eight major dust storms strike the Great Plains. New Deal begins.
1934	Drought spreads and becomes the worst ever, affecting three-quarters of the country.
1935	Robert Geiger coins the term "Dust Bowl." Black Sunday, the worst "black blizzard" of all, hits April 14. Experts announce that 850 million tons of topsoil have turned to dust and blown away from the southern plains.
1936	Okie exodus in full swing. California police patrol their state's borders with Arizona and Oregon to keep migrants out.
1937	President Roosevelt's Prairie Shelterbelt program gets underway.
1938	Department of Agriculture encourages farmers to change plowing methods to prevent soil erosion.
1939	Rain returns in the fall, ending the drought. World War II begins in Europe.
1940	President Roosevelt begins massive spending on armaments, finally pulling the country out of the Great Depression and creating jobs in the war industries.
1941	Japanese forces attack Pearl Harbor, bringing the United States into World War II.

Theodore Roosevelt
and the Rise of Modern America

ALA/YALSA Best Book for Young Adults

★ "Bully! Marrin does it again."
—*School Library Journal* (starred review)

Oh, Rats! The Story of Rats and People

ALSC Notable Children's Book ❖ CBC/NSTA Outstanding Tradebook

★ "Lively and informative . . . Impressive."
—*School Library Journal* (starred review)

Old Hickory:
Andrew Jackson and the American People

2005 James Madison Book Award

★ "More than a biography . . . [a] fine study."
—*School Library Journal* (starred review)

Dr. Jenner and the Speckled Monster:
The Search for the Smallpox Vaccine

CBC-NSTA Outstanding Science Tradebook

Riverbank Review Children's Book of Distinction

★ "A fascinating, eminently readable social history."
—*Booklist* (starred review)

George Washington
and the Founding of a Nation

Booklist Editors' Choice ❖ School Library Journal Best Book

ALA Best Book for Young Adults

"Marrin's impressive biography for young people is one well worth
poring over . . . One of the finest biographies about Washington to date."
—*The Boston Globe*

Commander in Chief:
Abraham Lincoln and the Civil War

ALA Best Book for Young Adults ❖ Booklist Editors' Choice

Jefferson Cup Award

★ "Marrin . . . once again demonstrates his ability to write
substantive books that never bore and that give readers new insights
into much-explored historical figures." —*Booklist* (starred review)

Sitting Bull and His World

ALA Best Book for Young Adults

Boston Globe-Horn Book Honor Award

Notable Social Studies Trade Book for Young People

Notable Book for a Global Society

★ "Marrin does an exceptional job of creating a full-length portrait."
—*Booklist* (starred review)

YEARS

OF

DUST

Albert Marrin

Years
of
Dust

THE STORY OF
The Dust Bowl

Dutton Children's Books

PHOTO CREDITS

ENDPAPERS:

"Denver to Chicago," Rand McNally and Co., 1921.
Courtesy of the University of Alabama Map Library.

PAGE i. HALF TITLE:

A migrant worker on a California highway, 1935.
Photograph by Dorothea Lange. From the Library of Congress.

PAGE ii-iii. TITLE SPREAD:

Dust storm near Beaver County, Oklahoma, on July 14, 1935.
From the Franklin D. Roosevelt Library.

Every attempt has been made to trace the ownership of all copyrighted
material and to secure necessary reprint permissions. In the event of any
question arising as to the use of reprinted material, the editor and the
publisher, while expressing regret for any inadvertent error, will be happy to
make necessary corrections in future printings. The publisher wishes to thank
those institutions who granted permission to reproduce works, and for their
kind cooperation in the realization of this book. Interior photo credits include:
Pages 1, 4, 52-53, 58-59 and 68-69, courtesy of the Franklin D. Roosevelt
Library; pages vii, 2, 3, 10, 11, 13-16, 18-27, 29, 32, 33, 35-39, 42-43, 44, 46-51,
54-57, 60, 62-67, 71, 73-97, 99-103, lower 104, 105, 107-109, 112, 116-118 and 122,
courtesy of the Library of Congress; pages 5, 9, 17, 28, 30-31 and 40, courtesy
of the Fred Hultstrand History in Pictures Collection, and pages 6-7 and 45,
courtesy of the F.A. Pazandak Photograph Collection, NDIRS-NDSU, Fargo;
pages 12, 41, 61, 70, 72, 98, upper 104, 110, 111, 114, 119, courtesy of USDA
National Resources Conservation Service; page 34 courtesy of NASA and STScl;
page 120 by Ryan Hagerty, courtesy of the US Fish & Wildlife Service;
page 121, courtesy of the Museum of History and Industry.

DUTTON CHILDREN'S BOOKS

A DIVISION OF PENGUIN YOUNG READERS GROUP

Published by the Penguin Group | Penguin Group (USA) Inc., 375 Hudson Street, New York, New York
10014, U.S.A. | Penguin Group (Canada), 90 Eglinton Avenue East, Suite 700, Toronto, Ontario M4P
2Y3, Canada (a division of Pearson Penguin Canada Inc.) | Penguin Books Ltd, 80 Strand, London
WC2R 0RL, England | Penguin Ireland, 25 St Stephen's Green, Dublin 2, Ireland (a division of Penguin
Books Ltd) | Penguin Group (Australia), 250 Camberwell Road, Camberwell, Victoria 3124, Australia
(a division of Pearson Australia Group Pty Ltd) | Penguin Books India Pvt Ltd, 11 Community Centre,
Panchsheel Park, New Delhi - 110 017, India | Penguin Group (NZ), 67 Apollo Drive, Rosedale, North
Shore 0632, New Zealand (a division of Pearson New Zealand Ltd.) | Penguin Books (South Africa)
(Pty) Ltd, 24 Sturdee Avenue, Rosebank, Johannesburg 2196, South Africa | Penguin Books Ltd,
Registered Offices: 80 Strand, London WC2R 0RL, England

Library of Congress Cataloging-in-Publication Data
Marrin, Albert.
Years of dust : the story of the Dust Bowl / Albert Marrin. — 1st ed.
p. cm.   Includes bibliographical references.
ISBN 978-0-525-42077-4
1. Great Plains—History—20th century—Juvenile literature. 2. Depressions—1929—Great Plains—
Juvenile literature. 3. Dust storms—Great Plains—History—20th century—Juvenile literature.
4. Droughts—Great Plains—History—20th century—Juvenile literature. 5. Farm life—Great Plains—
History—20th century—Juvenile literature. 6. Farmers—Great Plains—Social conditions—20th
century—Juvenile literature. 7. Great Plains—Social conditions—20th century—Juvenile
literature. 8. Dust Bowl Era, 1931–1939—Juvenile literature. I. Title.
F595.M343 2009   978'.032—dc22   2008013898

Published in the United States by Dutton Children's Books,
a division of Penguin Young Readers Group
345 Hudson Street, New York, New York 10014
www.penguin.com/youngreaders

DESIGNED BY HEATHER WOOD

Printed in China | First Edition | 10 9 8 7 6 5 4 3 2

Contents

Every blade of grass has its angel
that bends over it and whispers, "Grow, grow."

—The Talmud

Darkness At Noon

ST STORM APPROACHING SPEARMAN, TEX
APRIL 14 - 1935

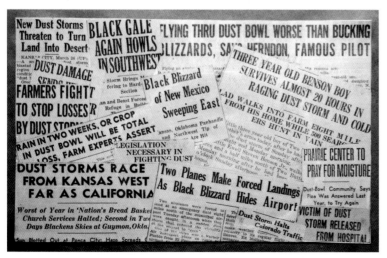

IN APRIL 1935, REPORTER ROBERT GEIGER set out by car across the Great Plains. As he headed east, heat waves made the air shimmer, causing him to squint. Temperatures rose to over one hundred degrees in the shade. There was nothing green visible in the fields; obviously, no rain had fallen for many weeks. Then, while driving across Oklahoma, Geiger encountered a "black blizzard," an immense dust storm. He had never imagined, let alone experienced, anything like it before. It was as if nature had gone insane.

At noon, darkness enveloped the earth. It seemed like an evil spirit had splashed an immense bucket of black paint across the sky. Within minutes, from horizon to horizon, the sun disappeared and noontime became "midnight." But such a midnight! There was no moon, no stars, no meteorites flashing across the heavens. Instead, billowing clouds of dust, some rising more than two miles into the air, whipped across the plains. Driven by howling winds, the clouds easily overtook speeding cars. As the dust fell back to earth, it drifted like dirty, crunchy snow, choking roads and bringing trains to a grinding halt. Worse, the dust buried crops and livestock, destroying farmers' homes and livelihoods.

The storm left Geiger shaken. Afterward, he interviewed some farmers. These old-timers, bony fellows with calloused hands and deep crease lines in their thin faces, seemed desperate. This was not the first dust storm they had experienced, nor, they reckoned, would it be the last. "Three little words," Geiger concluded, "achingly familiar on a Western farmer's tongue, rule life in the dust bowl of the continent—if it rains."[1]

Dust bowl! Geiger used the phrase as a way to make fun of gala sports events, like the Rose Bowl and Orange Bowl, two well-known football games. Geiger's phrase, however, took on a new meaning. It stuck, instantly grabbing the public's imagination. During the 1930s, as today, "Dust Bowl" became a dramatic term for the parts of the Great Plains stricken by the worst environmental disaster in American history.

Coming at the same time as the Great Depression, the dust storms not only ravaged the land, they tore at the human spirit. As the dust storms and the economic crisis continued, poet Archibald MacLeish wondered whether not only nature, but America itself, had failed. Could it be that our nation's best years were over? Could our future ever be as bright as our past? Five years after Geiger's drive into the dust, MacLeish wrote a book-length poem titled *The Land of the Free*. One verse showed his doubts about the future:

> **The meaning of the dust storms was that the grass was dead.**
> **We wonder whether the great American dream . . . is behind**
> **us now . . .**
> **We wonder if the liberty is done:**
> **The dreaming is finished.**[2]

Now we know that the dream is not finished. It continues, as vivid as ever. The Great Depression eased, and time proved that America would become stronger and richer than any nation in the history of

In this poster created by the Resettlement Administration in 1936, a farmer sits on a porch. Behind the distraught man a child stares through a window as a dust storm envelops the farm.

A young Oklahoma mother, age eighteen, penniless and stranded in Imperial Valley, California, about the year 1935.

the world. After nearly a decade, the rains returned to the Great Plains. The dust storms ended. The land blossomed again and the nation's spirits revived. The Dust Bowl became a bad memory.

This book aims to tell the story of the Dust Bowl disaster. It is really two stories. The first story focuses on ecology—the natural world of the Great Plains. The second story is about how people invited disaster by changing the ecology of the Great Plains; "assaulting" might be a better word. Both stories hold important lessons for us today because the Dust Bowl was caused less by natural forces than by people's abuse of the land.

The Dust Bowl story is not finished, nor can it ever be. If we do not learn from past mistakes, the future is as certain as tomorrow's sunrise. We must change our ways or there will be more dust bowls. The storms of the future may very well be even worse than the ones that ravaged the Great Plains in the 1930s.

The GREAT PLAINS World

There seemed to be nothing to see: no fences, no creeks or trees, no hills or fields. There was nothing but land: not a country at all, but the material out of which countries are made.

— Willa Cather, My Antonia (1918)

THERE IS NO WAY TO understand the Dust Bowl tragedy without first understanding the ecology of the Great Plains. Ecology is the branch of science that deals with the relationships between living beings and their physical environment. Mountains, rivers, lakes, deserts, jungles, and Arctic regions—to name a few—are all special environments. Each has unique life-forms that interact with each other and depend on each other to survive. So does the Great Plains.

A region of seemingly boundless open spaces, the plains lie at the heart of North America. Reaching southward from the Canadian provinces of Alberta, Saskatchewan, and Manitoba, they extend into northern Mexico. The plains also stretch eastward from the bases of the Rocky Mountains to the banks of the Mississippi and Missouri rivers.

Except for the Llano Estacado (Spanish for "Staked Plains") of Texas, the plains are not pancake-flat. They are wavelike, gently sloping downward from the Rockies toward the east. The plains have not always been dry land. Fossil seashells and fish show that they once formed the bed of a shallow inland sea. They owe their slope to

Previous page: Old-timers on the "Rosebud." Near White River, South Dakota, 1890.
Right: Three binders pulled by a Twin City "25" tractor in Fullerton, North Dakota, 1918. In the foreground is uncut grain and in the background are bundles of cut grain.

THE GREAT PLAINS & DUST BOWL REGIONS

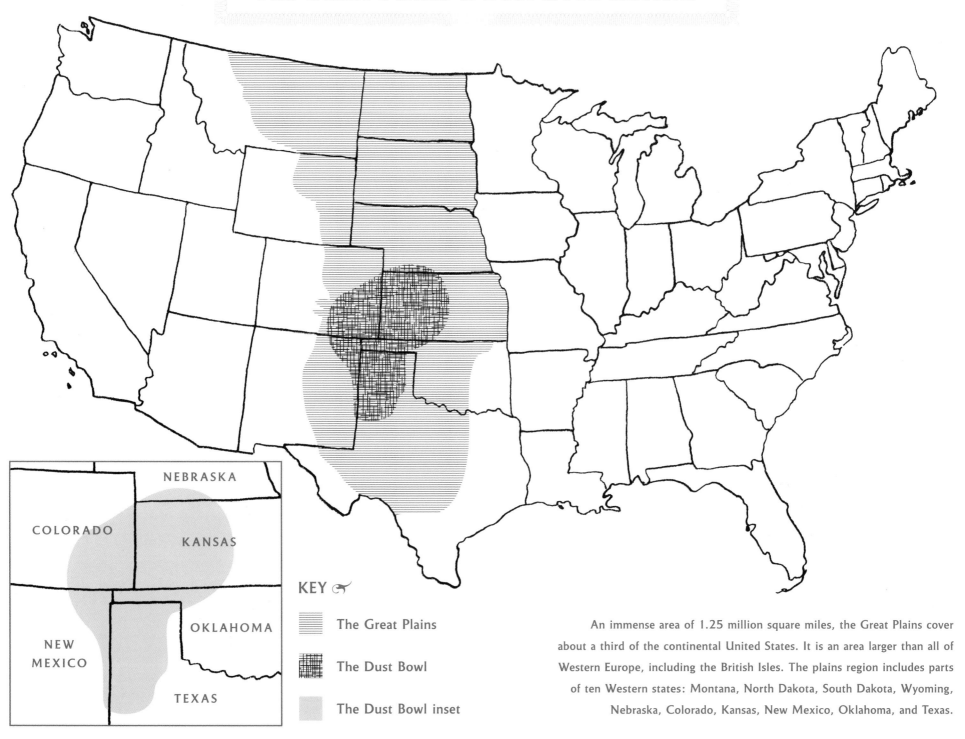

KEY

The Great Plains

The Dust Bowl

The Dust Bowl inset

NEBRASKA

COLORADO

KANSAS

NEW
MEXICO

OKLAHOMA

TEXAS

An immense area of 1.25 million square miles, the Great Plains cover about a third of the continental United States. It is an area larger than all of Western Europe, including the British Isles. The plains region includes parts of ten Western states: Montana, North Dakota, South Dakota, Wyoming, Nebraska, Colorado, Kansas, New Mexico, Oklahoma, and Texas.

the buildup of soil and stones washed down from the Rockies. Trees, mostly cottonwoods, grow along the banks of plains rivers. Otherwise, the region is treeless. In a few places, like the Black Hills of South Dakota, hills rise sharply from the surrounding countryside. Millions of years ago, when dinosaurs roamed the land, molten rock from the earth's core forced its way to the surface and solidified, forming the hills we see today.

The Great Plains is a place of extreme, violent weather. Weather can change suddenly from heavenly to horrid. With no trees to block it, the wind blows constantly. Often the wind reaches speeds seen nowhere else but at the seashore, blowing over one hundred miles an hour. Its moaning, whistling, and howling often tormented the first white settlers, people unused to such sounds. "A high wind is an awful thing," a woman wrote, "it wears you down, it nags at you day after day, it sounds like an invisible army, it fills you with terror as something invisible does." Now and then, the continual noise drove people out of their minds, even to suicide.[1]

Depending on the season, the wind brings scorching heat and numbing cold. Summer winds whip out of the Mexican deserts. Plains temperatures soar past one hundred degrees in the shade, and stay there for weeks, with no relief even at night. The dry heat is a killer. Streams vanish, leaving only a channel littered with round stones. Animals die of thirst. Plants shrivel up, as if caught in the blast of a gigantic furnace. In summertime, railroads might have to stop service because the heat expands the steel tracks, putting them out of alignment.

RIGHT: After the blizzard. A street scene in a Great Plains town. The group of men hold signs advertising local businesses. Photograph taken in Milton, North Dakota, April 13, 1893.

Winter on the Plains

Arctic winds lash the Great Plains in fall and winter. Called "northers," because they come out of the north, the fierce winds can make the thermometer drop fifty degrees in just a few minutes. Northers often bring blizzards. Even today, windows and doors must fit snugly to keep the fine wind-driven snow out of a house. In *The Plains of the Great West* (1877), army veteran Colonel Richard Irving Dodge wrote: "For a week each day will be clear [and] calm . . . No overcoat is needed, and the presence of winter is scarcely recognized. Then comes a storm; the icy wind cuts like a knife, no clothing seems to keep it from the person, and penetrating to every part it drags out every particle of vital heat, leaving but a stiffened corpse of him who is so unfortunate as to be exposed to it."

CATTLE IN A BLIZZARD ON THE PLAINS.—Drawn by Charles Graham from a Sketch by H. Worrall.—[See Page 135.]

Even today, wildfires ignited by lightning and driven by wind may burn until they run out of fuel or reach a stream. "It is a strange and terrible sight to see," wrote one settler, "all the fields a sea of fire. Quite often the scorching flames sweep everything along in their path—people, cattle, hay, fences. In dry weather with a strong wind the fire will race faster than the speediest horse."[2] To survive a plains fire, every creature in its path must run or fly, dig—or die. Yet the plains need periodic fires to stay healthy. Fire clears dead vegetation. The remaining ashes return as minerals to the soil, increasing its fertility.

Rainfall decides what, if anything, will grow. The Great Plains have what scientists call a semiarid climate, that is, a climate with light rainfall. Normally, the Great Plains region gets ten to twenty inches of rain a year, compared to twenty to forty inches in the Mississippi Valley and seventy-five inches in the Pacific Northwest. This is due in part to the Rocky Mountains. Their towering peaks form a wall, allowing few moisture-bearing clouds to drift eastward from the Pacific Ocean. Most moisture reaches the plains thanks to a low-level jet stream, a fast-moving current of winds that moves close to the earth's surface. This wind current goes from east to west across the Atlantic Ocean. It curves northward as it crosses the Gulf of Mexico, drawing in tropical moisture. Naturally, the farther north the low-level jet stream goes, the less moisture it bears, because it has already fallen as rain. For this reason, the northern plains are generally drier than the southern plains.

The Buffalo and the Indian

Plains Indian tribes like the Lakota (Sioux) and Cheyenne said everything they needed, except water for drinking and cooking, and wood for tepee poles, came from the buffalo. These hunters ate buffalo meat at every meal, several pounds at a time. Tanned buffalo hide became robes, blankets, caps, mittens, moccasins, leggings, shields, saddlebags, drums, and tepee walls. Their hair became rope, their tails flyswatters, their horns spoons, cups, and storage containers. Bones were shaped into needles, knife blades, spear points, war clubs, and awls to punch holes in leather. Boiled hooves made excellent glue, used to fasten arrowheads to their shafts. When it rained, buffalo dung stayed dry on the inside, making an all-weather fuel to warm a tepee or cook a meal.

Prairie Dog Town

Prairie dogs, a type of ground squirrel, live in vast underground "towns," or tunnels that extend for miles in all directions. A prairie dog town in Texas once took up 25,000 square miles and held an estimated 400 million animals—and there were hundreds like it. In all, scientists believe that as many as 25 billion prairie dogs once inhabited the plains. Soldiers on long patrols and pioneers sometimes ate prairie dogs. "He is not excellent eating," wrote Colonel Richard Irving Dodge, "but the young are as good as the common squirrel, and, when other meat is not to be had, they made no unwelcome addition to the bill of fare."

The Mississippi River is a natural dividing line for different types of plants, notably grasses. Since tall grasses such as big bluestem need more water, they grow east of the river. Because they need little water, short grasses grow west of the river. When white farmers first settled west of the river on the Great Plains, blue grama and buffalo grass were the chief short grasses. Called perennials, because they live for many years, these short grasses anchored themselves in the soil by a shallow network of tangled roots. This tough root mat, called "sod," easily absorbed rainwater. Equally important, sod held the soil in place, preventing it from washing or blowing away. Though fire burned the plains grasses, it could not reach their roots. Soon after the fire passed, fresh blades of grass would appear.

The Bible (Isaiah 40:6) says, "All flesh is grass." That is true. Animals, and people, depend on plants that chemically change the sun's radiant or light energy into food. The plains once teemed with plant-eating animals. Some, like jackrabbits, mice, and prairie dogs, were small. There were many larger animals, too. Scientists estimate that, before the arrival of white settlers, 25 million pronghorn antelopes bounded across the sea of grass. Nature designed the pronghorn for speed and endurance. With long, muscular legs, a large heart, and oversize lungs, it could travel for hours at thirty miles an hour.

The lord of the Great Plains was the American bison, or buffalo. When the first Europeans reached the New World, some 40 to 60 million buffalo roamed the region in their endless search for pasture. The buffalo was what ecologists call a keystone animal. In architecture, the keystone of an arch keeps the other stones in place.

OPPOSITE PAGE: Hunters stampeding a buffalo herd, January 2, 1917.

The Lord of the Plains

An adult buffalo eats up to thirty pounds of grass a day. The largest land animal in North America, a full-grown bull can stand six feet six inches tall at the shoulders, be ten feet from snout to rump, and weigh two thousand pounds. Adult cows are smaller, weighing just twelve hundred pounds. Buffalo once grazed in herds so large we can scarcely imagine them today. Easily excited, their stampedes shook the earth; their bellowing made it hard to get a night's sleep. Sometimes herds drank small rivers dry. As late as 1871, U.S. Army patrols found their way blocked by moving herds. Once, an officer reported, a herd took five days to pass and was fifty miles deep by ten miles wide. This herd was nothing special, just one of countless others that roamed the plains.

A keystone animal is one that other life-forms need to survive. For example, the hooves of grazing buffalo pushed seeds into the ground, where they sprouted and grew, becoming food for other herbivores. Another example is the prairie dog, which cannot live in tall grass. By grazing, buffalo kept the grass to the small creature's liking. This is important, for in digging their burrows, prairie dogs bring mineral-rich soil to the surface. In return, buffalo get needed salts by licking up dried urine around prairie dog holes. Buffalo dung—lumps of digested grass—served as breeding grounds for necessary insects and molds. Finally, after death, the buffalo's decaying body fertilized the soil and provided a feast for buzzards and bugs, coyotes and worms.

Carnivores (meat-eaters) thrived in the Great Plains environment. Golden eagles glided overhead, their keen eyes searching the ground for prey. Grizzly bears fed on living and dead animals of all sizes; a white traveler once counted 220 grizzlies in a day. Wolves ran in packs of fifty members or more. Seen from a distance, travelers said their light coats made them resemble flocks of sheep. Coyotes, rattlesnakes, and bobcats also had good hunting.

For sheer numbers, though, no plains creature equaled the grasshopper. Historical records describe what grasshopper outbreaks on the Great Plains were once like. Sometimes "hoppers" came in miles-wide clouds, billions upon billions of them, streaming across the sky. In her novel, *On the Banks of Plum Creek*, Laura Ingalls Wilder describes a grasshopper swarm in the mid-1880s:

> **. . . A cloud was over the sun. It was not like any cloud they had ever seen before. It was a cloud of something like snowflakes, and**

A plague of locusts fill the sky. This photograph was taken by the American Colony Photo Department in Palestine (present-day Israel and the West Bank). The region suffered a terrible plague of locusts from March through June of 1915. Locust plagues have been recorded in different places throughout the world since ancient times.

Grasshoppers: A Plains Plague

The word "locust" refers to the swarming phase of a short-horned grasshopper. Government scientists estimated that one particularly large swarm of grasshoppers was over one hundred miles long by one hundred miles wide. Creatures of summer, these insects thrive in hot, dry weather. Heat checks their natural enemies, which include bacteria, birds, and rodents. These insects also favor dry weather because abundant rain allows a certain type of fungus to grow which kills grasshoppers by releasing poisons into their bodies.

Plains grasshoppers can reach a length of four inches. The culprit, life-size.

thin and glittering. Light shone through each flickering particle.

There was no wind. The grasses were still and the hot air did not stir, but the edge of the cloud came across the sky faster than the wind. The hair stood up on [our dog] Jack's neck. All at once he made a frightful sound up at that cloud, a growl and a whine.

Plunk! Something hit Laura's head and fell to the ground. She looked down and saw the biggest grasshopper she had ever seen. . . .

The cloud was hailing grasshoppers. The cloud was grasshoppers. Their bodies hid the sun and made darkness. . . . The rasping whirring of their wings filled the whole air and they hit the ground and the house with the noise of a hailstorm.[3]

Wherever a grasshopper cloud set down, it cleared the ground of plant life. All you could hear was the sound of countless jaws CHOMP, CHOMP, CHOMPING until nothing remained to eat. Young children, caught outdoors, screamed in terror as the insects' claws caught in their hair and bodies wriggled into their clothing. On railroad tracks slippery with crushed grasshoppers, trains could not start or, worse, stop. Yet, since grasshopper jaws could not get at their roots, the native prairie grasses always grew back.

The Great Plains, then, was (and is) a harsh land. Despite the hardships, Americans still saw the plains as a place of opportunity. A place where, through hard work and good luck, they could build a better future. And so, in the nineteenth and early twentieth centuries, settlers flocked to the rolling grasslands west of the Mississippi. Unfortunately, the arrival of settlers would change the delicate ecology of the plains.

Conquering The Great Plains

When I was a schoolboy, my map of the United States showed . . .
a broad white blotch, upon which was printed in small capitals
"THE GREAT AMERICAN DESERT—UNEXPLORED."

— Colonel Richard Irving Dodge, explorer, 1880

EVEN BEFORE THE UNITED STATES won its independence from Great Britain in 1783, Daniel Boone and other pioneers were trekking across the Allegheny Mountains into Kentucky and Tennessee. Independence further encouraged the westward movement. The future, for countless people, lay beyond the settled areas along the Atlantic Coast. Land near the coast had already become scarce and expensive. But there was still cheap, abundant, fertile land in the West. There you could make a better life than your forefathers had ever imagined.

In 1803, President Thomas Jefferson made the Louisiana Purchase. An enormous tract of land between the Mississippi River and the Rocky Mountains suddenly became a part of the United States. But what had he really bought? People could only guess. So, in 1804, Jefferson sent Meriwether Lewis and William Clark to explore the new territory. Their journey proved it was possible to reach the Pacific Coast by traveling across the northern plains, then following the narrow passes through the Rockies.

In the journals they kept, expedition leaders and men described

18

PREVIOUS PAGE: Chicago and North Western passenger train no. 687, stuck in high snowdrifts in Dallas, South Dakota, on February 17, 1915. RIGHT: Railroad building on the Great Plains. This drawing by A. R. Waud appeared in the July 17, 1875, issue of <u>Harper's Weekly</u>.

Originally, when Americans spoke of the "West," they did not mean the Great Plains at all. The "West" simply meant the land between the Allegheny Mountains and the Mississippi River. That began to change during the presidency of Thomas Jefferson. In 1803, France sold the Louisiana Territory, all the land between the Mississippi and Missouri rivers and the Rocky Mountains, to the United States. It was a bargain. At a cost of fifteen million dollars, or three cents an acre, Jefferson doubled the country's size.

A portrait of President Thomas Jefferson.

the Great Plains as a world unto itself—vast, mysterious, and teeming with wildlife. Never having seen humans, most big herbivores had no fear of them. "The game is getting so plenty and tame in this country," Sergeant John Ordway wrote, "that some of the party clubbed them out of their way." Private Joseph Whitehouse noted, "The buffalo were so numerous and tame at a distance from us that some of [us] went up near enough to strike them with clubs."[1] The explorers, however, said nothing about whether pioneers could ever settle on the plains.

In 1819, the federal government sent an army officer, Major Stephen H. Long, to map various parts of the region. What Long saw convinced him that American settlers had no future in this wilderness. It was, he wrote in his official report, "almost wholly unfit for cultivation, and of course uninhabitable by a people depending upon agriculture for their subsistence." Flat, treeless, and dry, the grasslands were fit only for wild beasts and nomadic Indians. Along with his report, the major issued a wall map with the words "THE GREAT AMERICAN DESERT—UNEXPLORED" covering the region in large letters.[2]

For the next thirty years Americans ventured onto the plains with their horses and covered wagons. But they were always bound for somewhere else. Settlers headed for the fertile valleys of the Oregon Territory or, after 1849, the goldfields of the Golden State, California. For them, the Great American Desert was simply an obstacle to cross as swiftly and safely as possible.

Attitudes began to change when the Civil War ended in 1865 and

OPPOSITE PAGE: Major Stephen H. Long and members of his expedition meeting with a Pawnee council. Print from an engraving by John Heaviside Clark created in 1823.

London, Pub.d by Longman, Hurst, Rees, Orme, & Brown, 1823.

Pawnee Council

An Advanced Civilization?

"Kill, skin and sell until the buffaloes are exterminated," General Phil Sheridan, a Civil War hero, told Texans in 1875. "Then your prairie can be covered with speckled cattle and the festive cowboy . . . [will be the] forerunner of an advanced civilization."[3]

On the opposite page, Wyoming cowboy and rodeo star Harry "Hoot" Jones rides the previously unbridled bronco, Silver City, during the 1910 Cheyenne Frontier Days festival. Photographs from the festival showing Jones's rodeo skills were admired throughout the world. They may have inspired the symbol, found on state license plates and quarters, for Wyoming—the silhouette of a cowboy on a bucking horse.

railroads started to flourish. One plains state, Texas, had fought on the Confederate side of the war. Texas was cattle country. For generations, first Spaniards, then Mexicans, and finally settlers from the United States had raised cattle on Texas short grasses. Americans wanted Texas beef, but it was hard to get it to them. While railroads expanded in the East, they had yet to reach the Great Plains. Nevertheless, ranchers walked a few small herds to market in California and New Orleans on the Gulf of Mexico. Ranchers owned the herds. Cowboys, hired men who herded cattle on horseback, did the actual work.

After the Civil War, the federal government wanted to tie the country together with railroads. Railroads allowed ranchers to ship their cattle, worth four dollars a head in Texas, to New York and other cities where they sold for forty dollars a head. In doing so, ranchers struck mankind's first serious blow to the ecology of the Great Plains.

As Texas ranchers grew rich, others decided to expand the "Cattle Kingdom" into Montana and the Dakotas on the northern plains. Yet two obstacles barred their way: the buffalo and the Indians. Buffalo were uneconomical—at least white settlers thought so. Nicknamed "stinkers," every year they ate millions of tons of grass needed to feed the growing cattle herds. Indian tribes, however, had ancient traditions as buffalo hunters. They would fight to preserve the herds that made their way of life possible. "Progress," as white people saw it, demanded that both the buffalo and the Indians should go.

Professional hunters armed with high-powered rifles slaughtered buffalo for their hides, which factories turned into all sorts of leather products. Within a decade, bands of hunters cleared the Great Plains

An Oglala Sioux known as Picket Pin holds a buffalo skull, a sacred relic among the plains tribes. Photograph taken by Edward S. Curtis in 1907.

Opposite page: "Slaughtered for the Hide." This engraving appeared on the cover of Harper's Weekly (the Journal of Civilization) on December 12, 1874. It shows men skinning buffalos.

of all but a few hundred buffalo. In places, you could walk on their rotting carcasses for hundreds of yards without setting foot on the ground. Theodore Roosevelt, a future president, wrote from his ranch in North Dakota:

> **On those portions where the [buffalo] herds made their last stand, the carcasses, dried in the clear, high air, or the mouldering skeletons, abound. . . . These carcasses were in sight from every hillock, often lying over the ground so thickly that several score could be seen at once. A ranchman who . . . had made a journey of a thousand miles across northern Montana . . . told me that, to use his own expression, during the whole distance he was never out of sight of a dead buffalo, and never in sight of a live one.[4]**

With the buffalo all but gone, the U.S. Army used force and starvation to drive the Indian tribes onto reservations.

By the 1880s, ranching flourished on the southern and northern plains, but at great cost to the environment. Despite the buffalo's vast numbers, they did not damage the grasslands. The roaming herds ate the grass, dropped their dung, and moved on to fresh pasture. Their manure fertilized the soil. Their sharp hooves broke the ground, letting in air and moisture. The shape of a buffalo's jaw allowed it to bite only to a few inches above the ground, so the grass recovered quickly. It was as if nature had designed the buffalo to preserve the grasslands.

Cattle were different. For one, they could not move on, but had to graze in a confined space. This meant that, over time, their hooves compacted the soil, reducing its ability to absorb and hold water. In-

Ornery Buffalo Hunters

Buffalo hunting was not for the squeamish. Hunters were often social outcasts. Even the army did not want them. Many refused to give their names, preferring only nicknames like Shoot-'em-up Mike, Shotgun Collins, and Prairie Dog Jake. Shaggy and bearded, they stank to high heaven and swarmed with "bed rabbits" (fleas). A traveler described the typical hunter: "He had long hair and was the dirtiest, greasiest, and smokiest mortal I had ever seen." Yet, another noted, hunters were tough customers. Unless a hunter was "head, neck, or gut shot, he was too damn stubborn and ornery to die!"[5]

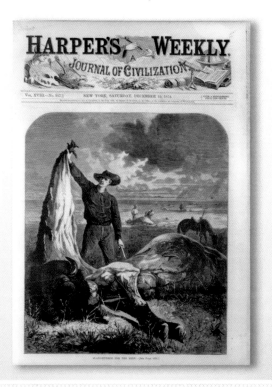

stead of sinking into the hardened ground, rainwater ran off, causing erosion—that is, the gradual wearing away of the soil. Also, cattle have jaws designed to bite grasses down to their roots, never allowing the plants to recover.

Ranchers made things even worse by destroying animals they considered pests. Since "varmints"—grizzlies, wolves, coyotes—killed cattle, ranchers shot them, including pregnant females and the young. Eagles swooped down to take newborn calves, so ranchers shot them, too. With the big predators gone, smaller herbivores multiplied. For example, prairie dogs ate ever-larger amounts of grass. Ranchers then poisoned entire prairie dog towns, thus reducing the soil's fertility, since prairie dogs helped to keep the sod healthy. Before long, large areas of rangeland dried up, unable to support anything but tumbleweed.

A crisis came in the winter of 1886–87. Westerners still call it the "Big Die-Up." That fall, all signs pointed to a severe winter ahead. Along streams, beavers and muskrats grew their fur heavier than usual. Trees grew thicker and tougher bark. Migrating birds flew south early, and white arctic owls appeared for the first time on record. Then, as monster blizzards struck the Great Plains from Canada to Texas, the wind brought snow.

Snow began falling on November 16. It continued, on and off, for over a hundred days, until late February. Sometimes temperatures fell to minus sixty-eight degrees, winds roared at sixty miles an hour, and snow fell at the rate of an inch an hour. It fell, a rancher re-

OPPOSITE PAGE: General Nelson A. Miles and staff viewing a large Lakota (Sioux) Indian Camp. Photograph taken near Pine Ridge, South Dakota, on January 16, 1891. RIGHT: "In a blizzard," from a painting by Frank Feller, c. 1900. Getting caught outdoors in a plains blizzard was usually fatal.

Losing Your Way

A North Dakota rancher recalled getting caught outdoors in a blizzard: "Barns and [hay] stacks were literally covered with drifting snow. . . . Persons lost upon the prairie were almost certain to meet death, unless familiar with the nature of these storms. . . . I learned of many instances where persons were lost in trying to go from the house to the barn, and of other instances where cords were fastened to the house so that, if the barn should be missed, by holding on to the cord the house could be found again."[6]

The Last Buffalo

The title of this photograph is "The Last Buffalo Killed in North Dakota." It was taken in Casselton, North Dakota, in January 1907. Men and boys in winter coats stand behind the captive animal. A man on the right holds a rope tied around the animal's horns. A copy of the photograph was sent to the president. He replied: "My dear Mr. Lynch: I thank you for your gift, and appreciate it. And yet I am really sorry that you had to kill that buffalo bull. I am surprised that there should have been no market for him in the different parks and museums of this country, for I would have thought there would be plenty of people who would like to have him. With regard and thanks, I am, Sincerely yours, Theodore Roosevelt"—January 28, 1907.[9]

Last Buffalo Killed IN N.D. At CASSELTON Jan 07.

called, "like a tornado of pure white dust or very fine sand, icy cold, and stinging like a whiplash. . . . The blizzard abated, but the icy cold did not; another blizzard came, and another and another."[7]

Going outdoors in a blizzard was often deadly. It became a total whiteout, a condition in which falling, blowing, and drifting snow reduce visibility to zero. Landmarks disappeared in the blinding snow. Riders and their mounts fell over the edges of snow-filled ravines, got buried, and died. A drunken cowboy left a saloon and froze stiff. Since the ground was too hard to dig a grave, friends stood him up and hung a lantern on him to help others find their way.

Cattle suffered a worse fate than people. The poor animals stood belly-deep in snowdrifts, eyelids frozen shut, icicles dangling from muzzles. Thousands starved and froze where they stood. Come spring, Dakota rancher Theodore Roosevelt found the land "a mere barren waste; not a green thing could be seen; the dead grass eaten off till the country looked as if it had been shaved by a razor."[8] The stench of rotting flesh filled the air. Ranchers had lost between 40 and 90 percent of their livestock. Hundreds of small outfits went broke. The survivors learned their lesson. From then on, they kept smaller herds and stored hay for the winter.

In the decades that followed, farmers soon claimed the land ranchers had abandoned, and millions more acres besides. The farmers would change the very nature of the grasslands and set the stage for the tragedy of the Dust Bowl.

The Coming of the Farmers

The waning years of the nineteenth century witnessed the greatest movement of peoples in the history of the United States. Millions of farmers, held back . . . by the forbidding features of the Great Plains, surged westward. . . .

— RAY ALLEN BILLINGTON, HISTORIAN OF THE AMERICAN WEST

MOST RANCHERS DID NOT OWN the land on which their cattle grazed. They called it "free range," because it belonged to the federal government and was used free of charge. Only after the Big Die-Up did ranchers buy some choice grazing land from the government.

The federal government was (and still is) the nation's largest land-owner. In 1862, as the Civil War raged, Congress passed the Home-stead Act to encourage settlement in the West. This law offered 160 acres of public land to any citizen, or immigrant intending to become a citizen, of the United States. All one had to do was pay a ten-dollar registration fee, live on the land for five years, and "improve" it by building a house or barn and farming it. Settlers could also buy as much land as they pleased for $1.25 an acre. Rather than file a home-stead claim, many bought their land directly from the government or a railroad company. That way the land became theirs immediately, and they could do whatever they wished with it.

Selling Great Plains lands became big business. Eager to cash in, railroads created land departments. Every railroad had agents, called "boosters," in seaports like New York City. The boosters

PREVIOUS PAGE: Three horses pull a hand plow.
RIGHT: Christ Nelson sod house and Soper Post Office, North Dakota, 1896. The Soper Post Office was established on June 11, 1888, and closed on October 15, 1906. Notice the grass growing on the roof.

For Want of Rain

Scientists believe the plains have suffered droughts for at least ten thousand years. One drought lasted twenty-three years, from 1276 to 1299, and affected the Anasazi people of southwestern Colorado. These Native American farmers grew corn, cotton, beans, and squash. They built their homes into the sides of cliffs in what is today Mesa Verde National Park. The drought drove the Anasazi away, but it is unclear where they went. Left to the wind and the owls, their cliff dwellings remained untouched until modern times. Today, Mesa Verde National Park is a favorite tourist destination. The largest structure, called Cliff Palace, has more than two hundred storage and living rooms, which housed upward of three hundred people. Cliff Palace also has many kivas, underground rooms in which Anasazi gathered for religious ceremonies.

greeted immigrants, arranged credit, and took them to the plains by train. Special agents, men who made a good impression and had the gift of gab, appeared in Europe. In speeches, handbills, and posters they touted the former Great American Desert as "The Garden of the West." It was a wonderland, they said, where colorful birds "warble musical challenges to each other amid the rich foliage of the sweet-bay and mango trees." One need hardly raise a sweat to make a fortune. "Settling on the prairie which is ready for the plow, is different from plunging into a region covered with timber. Nature seems to have provided protection for man and beast; all that is required is diligent labor and economy to ensure an early reward." The boosters were convincing. Between 1870 and 1890, over two million Europeans, mostly Germans and Scandinavians, settled on the plains.[1]

Land agents did not mention that the plains were prone to periodic droughts. While crossing the Gulf of Mexico, the low-level jet stream may weaken. As it does, it shifts southward so that little rain, if any, reaches the grasslands west of the Mississippi. Most droughts have lasted a year or two, a few for decades. Dry spells on the Great Plains are always hot spells, too. While the heat once turned the tough mat of native grasses brown, the grass roots still held the topsoil in place. Some land was unprotected by grass even before the ranchers and farmers arrived. This bare land spawned what settlers called "sand blows," or dust storms.

Wind is one of nature's most powerful forces, able, literally, to reshape the land. Blowing at thirty miles an hour, wind can separate particles of dry, unprotected soil from each other. Blowing at forty

OPPOSITE PAGE: A stock watering hole in Cimarron County, Oklahoma, in 1936, during the height of the Dust Bowl. The water hole is almost completely covered by shifting topsoil.

Unearthly Dust Storms

Mars is called the "Red Planet" because its surface is naturally covered with red sand and dust. At various times of the year, Martian winds kick up dust storms that dwarf any seen on Earth. Unlike such storms on our planet, Martian dust storms do not just come and go. Often they last for weeks, even months. In July 2001, the National Aeronautics and Space Administration (NASA) reported the biggest dust storm ever recorded anywhere. It covered the entire surface of Mars, and was so big that amateur astronomers with simple telescopes could see it clearly from Earth. Astronomer Phil Christiansen puts the storm into perspective: "Although Mars is smaller than Earth, its surface area equals the sum of all the continents on our planet. Imagine a dust storm on Earth that blanketed every continent at once."[3]

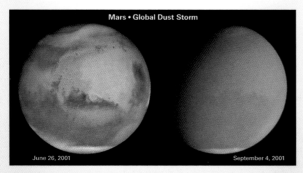

These Hubble Space Telescope images show the Red Planet before (left) and during (right) the great Martian dust storm of 2001.

miles an hour or more, it picks up soil particles and drives them against others, dislodging them in turn and forming a dust cloud. In 1880, well before the crisis of the Dust Bowl, a Wichita, Kansas, newspaper described what a typical dust storm felt like. "This wind for a week has just . . . howled and screeched and snorted. . . . Dust, grit, and sand everywhere—in your victuals, up your nose, down your back, between your toes. . . . Out of doors people communicate by signs. When they would talk they must retire to some room without windows or a crack, pull out their ear plugs and wash their mouths."[2]

The point is, dust storms are and always have been normal on the plains. Some places, like Nebraska, have giant sand dunes, really sand mountains formed millions of years ago. Only their grass covering keeps the dunes from "migrating," or moving where the wind blows them.

Luckily, settlers who came in the 1880s and 1890s arrived at a good time. Thanks to the jet stream, rain was plentiful. The newcomers jumped to the conclusion that it would always be so. They had no idea that, inevitably, the moisture-bearing wind would change direction. When it did, their farming methods would turn natural droughts and dust storms into something abnormal: the ferocious "black blizzards" of the Dust Bowl.

Before they could "put in," or plant a crop, new settlers had to provide for their basic needs. Water was essential; nothing can live without it. In Europe and the Eastern United States, water was plentiful. One had only to take it from a river or stream, or dig a shallow well, say fifty feet deep, and drop a bucket at the end of a rope.

Out on the grasslands, however, getting water was a serious challenge. Farmers might have to go down one hundred feet or more before reaching water. At first, they dug by hand, a tedious job shared by the whole family. By the early twentieth century, traveling well diggers, charging twenty cents a foot, used steam-powered drilling machines to bore into the Ogallala Aquifer, a vast underground reservoir. To bring water to the surface, they harnessed a free source of power, the wind. The prairie windmill, an inexpensive device of wood and iron, was a reliable water pump. Kept in small storage tanks, the water was used for cooking, washing, and drinking by people and for livestock. For watering their crops, however, farmers depended on rainfall.

Shelter was as important as water. In the forested eastern states, the early settlers built log cabins. On the treeless plains, however, they relied on a very different material: "prairie marble." Using a sledlike tool with a long blade on each side, settlers cut strips of sod a yard long and a foot wide. Called "bricks," these strips were fashioned into walls two feet thick and a roof several inches thick. Well insulated against extreme weather, the sod house, or "soddie," kept out the searing summer heat and the frigid blasts of winter northers. Yet it had drawbacks. Always dark and musty, heavy rain caused leaks, turning the soddie's earthen floor to mud. Often spiders and insects crawled out of the sod, and settlers had to pour boiling water on the walls to kill them. These crude homes served until the settler could save enough to buy lumber, brought by railroad, for a frame house.

To prepare the land for planting, the plains farmer had literally to break it open, which earned him the nickname "sodbuster." Most did this with the moldboard plow. Invented a thousand years ago in

The Reservoir Under the Plains

The Ogallala Aquifer is the major source of water in the Great Plains region. An aquifer is a layer of earth, sand, or porous rock that contains water. Since an aquifer lies between two layers of clay or solid rock, it collects surface water. The Ogallala Aquifer underlies the land from South Dakota to Texas. Formed by melting glaciers at the end of the Ice Age, fifteen thousand years ago, it has always been a dependable source of water. Recently, however, extensive farming has seriously drawn down the water supply.

Digging a well for families moving into Farm Security Administration houses in South Carolina, 1941.

Europe, the plow had a curved iron plate (moldboard) above the share or cutting blade. As the share sliced through the tough grass roots, the moldboard raised the sod and turned it over. Plowing was hard work, but worth the effort. Plains soil was so fertile, a settler wrote, that "it looked like chocolate where the plow turned the sod."[4] Those who could afford thirty-five dollars, no small sum in the 1890s, used the horse-drawn sulky or riding plow. Each sulky came with a seed container, allowing for plowing and planting in the same operation.

The riding plow belonged to a family of laborsaving devices that plains settlers used. Among these was a special machine used to harvest wheat, the chief plains crop. The farmer sat on a seat behind the horses pulling his Marsh Harvester. As it moved through the field, the Marsh's sharp blades cut the wheat so that it landed on an attached platform. Family members or hired men walking beside the platform tied the wheat into bundles, or sheaves, with rope.

The real breakthrough in farm machinery came with the tractor and the combine. A tractor is a machine used for traction—for drawing, towing, or pulling something that cannot move on its own. Invented in England in the 1700s, stationary "traction engines" at mines hauled cars laden with coal to the surface. In the first years of the twentieth century, Americans began building farm tractors around steam engines. Tractors suited the plains perfectly. A tractor could pull a disk plow. This had a series of iron disks that carved furrows in a fraction of the time needed by the old moldboard and sitting plows. The combine, as its name suggests, combines two tasks in a single machine. Pulled by a tractor, it cuts and threshes grain while moving over a field.

OPPOSITE PAGE: Combined harvester and thresher drawn by a large team of horses, c. 1903.

Farm Machinery Developments

The word thresh comes from "thrash"—to beat. For ages, after harvesting, farmers threshed grain with a handheld flail. This was a wooden handle with a short stick attached at one end by a leather thong so that it swung freely. Threshing by hand was hard and time-consuming. Yet, if not done promptly, rain might cause the sheaves to rot. By the late 1800s, horse-drawn machines were doing the job with metal flails. Most farmers did not own one. Instead, for a fee, a professional traveled around a district with his thresher and work crew after the harvest.

A family in Belpre, Kansas, stands proudly by a William Phillips steam plow, c. 1910. Steam plows would shortly give way to gasoline-powered tractors.

Corralling the Prairie

Since the plains lacked wood for fencing, farmers relied on mass-produced barbed wire. An easy to build "bob wahr" fence took up little space, withstood high winds, and did not allow snowdrifts to form around it. Invented by an Illinois farmer and patented in 1874, cheap barbed wire fencing made it possible for cattle owners to enclose much larger areas of grassland, and graze more head of cattle, than ever before.

A farmer puts up a barbed wire fence in El Indio, Texas, in 1939.

Thanks to these advances in machinery, farming became easier, faster, and more efficient. Able to cultivate more land than could ever have been possible with hand tools, the plains farmer became more productive than any in history. The bare numbers tell an amazing story. Take wheat, the main crop grown on the plains. In 1800, it took 373 worker-hours to produce 100 bushels of wheat. By 1900, it took just 108 worker-hours to produce the same number of bushels. Farmers did not eat most of the wheat, corn, and oats they grew. These were cash crops, grown chiefly for sale to others. Most cash crops were exported to Europe for sale as flour and animal feed. In America, millers sold flour to city bakeries, which turned it into bread. With the money plains farmers earned, they paid their debts and bought whatever city-made manufactured goods they needed. This included everything from machine-made nails to clothing made in factories in standard sizes and colors. Thus, the farmers' livelihood depended on the needs and work of people far away, whose names they never knew.

Despite laborsaving machinery, plains farmers had plenty to keep them busy. Farming was a family enterprise, and all but infants in the cradle had to pitch in for it to succeed. During planting and harvesting, men worked in the fields. At other times, they built or repaired farm buildings, tended the livestock, and kept the barbed wire fences in order.

Women worked as hard as their menfolk. Day in and day out, from dawn to bedtime, the farmer's wife kept to an unchanging routine. She cooked, baked, washed, ironed, sewed, churned cream for butter, tended her garden, and canned fruits and vegetables.

Since doctors were miles away in town, farm women often treated their family's ills. Patent medicines, or medicines sold without a doctor's prescription, were available in groceries and from mail-order firms. A variety of home remedies were also used. To clear the throat and chest of phlegm, for example, the woman made her patient suck on a lump of sugar laced with turpentine. To ease swollen glands, she wrapped a towel soaked with kerosene and lard around the patient's throat. In blistering-hot weather, she doled out sassafras tea to "thin" the blood. To prevent infection, she daubed cuts and bruises with homemade corn whiskey. Now and then, she delivered a neighbor's baby.

Children had their chores, too. Almost from the day they could walk, parents put their children to light tasks such as feeding the chickens. When they reached the age of nine or so, their parents expected children to milk the cows, haul buckets of water from the well, and generally pitch in. On foot or horseback, children went to the local one-room schoolhouse, nearly always several miles away. There, all grades learned the three R's—reading, 'riting, and 'rithmetic—together.

Farmers seldom traveled farther than the nearest town. Until early in the twentieth century, they went on horseback or in horse-drawn wagons. Then came the automobile. At first, farmers resented the motorcar. This smoke-spewing monster, rattling along at the breakneck speed of twenty miles an hour, scared the livestock. Yet it cost less than a big wagon and a team of horses. Henry Ford, the father of mass production, gave farmers an offer too tempting to refuse. Ford charged $295 for his Model T "Tin Lizzie." The vehicle, he said, came

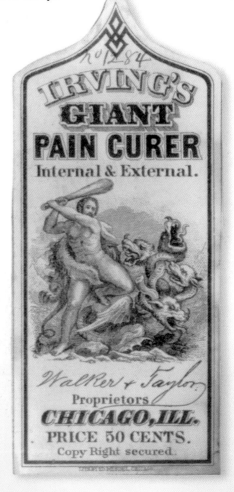

Relief in a Bottle

In the early 1900s, a host of patent medicines advertised as "soothing syrups," "energizing tonics," and "healing potions" contained habit-forming drugs such as opium and cocaine. Nicknamed "Black Bottle," one medicine contained a small amount of opium to soothe teething infants so their parents could get a full night's sleep.

Let's Go for a Spin

Eva, Hazel, Nettie, Rose, Ida, and Clarence Baker in Osnabrock, North Dakota, c. 1909. Five sisters sit in an open Model T Ford, each with scarves over their hair. Their brother, Clarence, sits on the running board. Their parents, Henry Baker and Euphemia Houston, came to North Dakota in 1885 to homestead. They raised a family of seven children and were successful farmers.[5] Note the neatly painted wooden house in the background, made from lumber most likely brought by railroad to the plains. The new car is parked on grass rather than a paved driveway and sits high off the ground. Early cars had to sit high so that they could make their way over rough country roads.

in any color you wanted, provided it was black. Better yet, Ford's engineers designed cars with high frames for travel over unpaved country roads. Soon, successful farmers were buying cars.

"Going to town" was a treat for the whole family. By the 1920s, hundreds of towns dotted the plains. Usually built along railroad lines, they seemed alike, as if formed by the same "cookie cutter." Plains towns were small, usually having fewer than a thousand inhabitants. Their tallest structures were the grain elevators, tile-covered towers filled with grain, awaiting shipment beside the railroad tracks. Most towns had one paved street—Main Street. There visitors found the post office, lumberyard, general store, bank, druggist, lawyer, dentist's and doctor's offices. A town might also have a hotel, movie house, soda fountain, its own newspaper, and telephone line. Many customers shared a telephone line. Although each receiver had its unique "ring," other customers could pick up their receivers and listen to the conversation.

The Fourth of July was the most exciting day of the year. Farmers came from miles around to socialize while celebrating their country's independence with horseshoe-pitching contests, baseball games, fireworks, and a parade down Main Street. It was, most agreed, good to be a farmer on the Great Plains. Yet, as they spoke, their world was changing. The changes would not be good for most people, but would be especially hard on farmers.

In Hard Times

Whatsoever a man soweth, that shall he also reap.

— BIBLE (GALATIANS 6:7)

THE OUTBREAK OF THE FIRST World War in Europe in 1914 made American agriculture more profitable than ever. In the struggle between the Allies (Great Britain, France, Russia, Belgium, Italy) and the Central Powers (Germany, Austria-Hungary, Turkey), European farms became battlefields. Not only did armies fight in the countryside, forcing farmers to flee, but food became as vital to victory as guns and bullets. To prevent the Allies from getting food from overseas, Germany unleashed its submarine fleet, with terrifying results. Torpedoes sent hundreds of Allied merchantmen to the bottom of the Atlantic Ocean. The undersea raiders did so much damage that, by April 1917, Great Britain had only a six-week supply of food on hand. That same month, the U.S. Congress declared war on Germany for sinking American ships bound for Allied ports.

Even before German submarine attacks brought the United States into the war, America had been the Allies' "breadbasket," their chief food supplier. Now that the United States had joined the Allies, America had to meet both European food needs and its own to win the war. But how?

PREVIOUS PAGE: A shack in Oklahoma City's Hooverville. Metal advertising signs are nailed together to form the wall on the right. RIGHT: A breadline beside New York's Brooklyn Bridge approach during the Great Depression, c. 1935.

President Herbert Hoover

Herbert Hoover, a wealthy engineer, had already organized relief efforts for the civilians of war-torn Belgium. Thanks to Hoover's quick action in 1914, American food kept many thousands of innocent Belgians from starving.

Now, with America in the war, Hoover took charge of the effort to get Americans to save food and produce even more food. He launched a propaganda campaign to remind people of their patriotic duty. "Save food!" he demanded in posters, newspaper advertisements, and slogans. "Wheat will win the war!"

To encourage wheat production, Congress passed the Food Control Act of 1917. By law, the price of a bushel of wheat leaped from 93 cents to $2.20. Plains farmers saw a marvelous opportunity, and they took it. To make more money, they needed more land and the latest machines—tractors and combines—to work it. To buy the machinery, however, they first had to go into debt. Across the plains, farmers went to local bankers for mortgages. A mortgage is a special type of loan. In return for money, borrowers give lenders *collateral*, or legal ownership of their property. Should the borrower *default*, be unable to repay the loan when due, the lender could *foreclose*, which meant taking the property. So, by borrowing, farmers took advantage of an opportunity, but also took a terrific gamble. In time, losing that gamble would cost many families their land, homes, and livelihoods.

At first, the gamble seemed to pay off. During the war years, plains farmers were blessed with glorious weather and high profits. Prosperity continued even after the Allied victory in November 1918.

OPPOSITE PAGE: Rear view of disking with a Big 4 tractor, pulling seven six-foot disks. Probably in North Dakota, c. 1910-1915.

Although peace returned, Europe still needed American food. By the early 1920s, however, European agriculture had recovered. The overseas market for American food, particularly wheat, shrank. Worse, with production still soaring in the plains states, farmers were growing more than American consumers needed. Food prices fell.

What to do? Rather than cut production to keep prices high, farmers did the opposite. It was like trying to run faster and faster just to stay in place. Hoping to offset falling prices by plowing and planting more, farmers went deeper into debt to buy more land and equipment. With gasoline-powered tractors, a recent invention, they attacked the grasslands in what became known as the "Great Plow-Up." By the late 1920s, another 5,260,000 acres of grassland were lost to the plow, an area nearly seven times the size of the state of Rhode Island. Most of this ground went to shallow-rooted wheat.

As farm prices continued to fall, banks foreclosed when owners defaulted on their mortgage payments. If they acted in time, farmers might avoid foreclosure by selling out to wealthier neighbors. Those who sold out drifted away from farming altogether, or became tenants and sharecroppers. Tenant farmers rented their land for hard cash, while sharecroppers gave landowners a share of the harvest as rent. Neither had any rights to the land; the owner could throw them out at any time and for any, or no, reason.

Often the wealthiest did not own family farms—were not farmers at all. During the 1920s, big-city businessmen saw a chance to make a bundle of money quickly. In Texas, for example, movie producer

LEFT: Auction at a farm near New Hradec, North Dakota, in July, 1936.
OPPOSITE PAGE: A homeless ex-farmer and his children in a Hooverville in Circleville, Ohio, 1938. Many families lost their homes to foreclosure during the Great Depression.

Woody Guthrie

Woodrow Wilson Guthrie (1912–1967) was born in Oklahoma. At about the age of sixteen, "Woody," as everyone called him, left home to spend the greater part of his life roaming the country. During his travels, Woody became a folksinger and composer. He wrote about a thousand songs in all, including the ever-popular "So Long, It's Been Good to Know You" and "This Land Is Your Land." His songs dealt with ordinary people, their hopes and hardships, and what life was like for them during the Great Depression. Woody told his life story in a 1943 book, *Bound for Glory*.

Hickman Price bought fifty-four square miles of farmland and unbroken grassland. With scores of hired workers, Price ran his fleet of tractors and disk plows steadily, even at night, and twenty-five combines at harvest time.[1] Like Henry Ford, who made his fortune by selling immense numbers of motorcars cheaply, Price and those like him made fortunes selling lots of wheat cheaply. They had, in effect, created giant factory farms.

Starting in 1929, the entire U.S. economy took the steepest downturn in the nation's history. Known as the Great Depression, historians still disagree on its causes. What is clear is that the downturn began in October, right after prices on the New York Stock Exchange collapsed. In the decade that followed, businesses went broke and factories closed their gates. As many as 14 million Americans, or one in four workers, became jobless. Many would not get another full-time job for years. With Americans unable to buy foreign goods, the Depression spread overseas, harming all of America's trading partners.

Depression-era America was a haunted land. In the cities, beggars roamed the streets. Millions of families, unable to meet mortgage or rent payments, became homeless. Herbert Hoover, who had become president the year before the stock market "crash," was the most hated person in the country. Desperate people, terrified of what the future held for themselves and their families, blamed him personally for their troubles. Wherever he appeared, crowds raised their fists and chanted, "Hang Hoover! Hang Hoover! Hang Hoover!"

Shanty towns of men, women, and children who had lost their homes sprang up all over America. These camps, composed of shacks crudely built from scavenged wood, metal, and cardboard, were derisively dubbed "Hoovervilles." There was an infamous Hooverville in New York City's Central Park and another holding many Dust Bowl refugees in Oklahoma City. The largest one, built on vacant land outside of Washington D.C., held over fifteen thousand people at its peak. With no electricity, plumbing, or reliable heat, conditions in these settlements were deplorable.

The hungry waited hours in line for meager handouts at soup kitchens run by charities. Others barely managed to stay alive. In describing what he called the "American Earthquake," writer Edmund Wilson told of an elderly lady who always took off her eyeglasses to avoid seeing the maggots swarming over the garbage she ate. Starvation claimed many victims. Four New York hospitals reported ninety-five starvation deaths within a twelve-month period.

The Depression years dealt farmers a double dose of misery. Since the unemployed had little money to spend, food prices fell further. As city incomes shrank, even more farm families, unable to meet their mortgage payments, lost everything in foreclosures. Of course, farmers resented bankers for seizing their property. After all, they felt, a family that invested its sweat and blood in a farm had a stronger claim to it than a banker, who only had words scribbled on a mortgage paper. Bankers, farmers said, were "banksters," criminals worse than gangsters. Many went further; they saw bank robbers as heroes.

In "The Ballad of Pretty Boy Floyd," folksinger Woody Guthrie turned a real-life Oklahoma bank robber into a modern-day Robin Hood, who paid farmers' mortgages with his loot:

Pretty Boy Floyd

Pretty Boy (real name Charles Arthur Floyd) and other western bandits, like Bonnie Parker and Clyde Barrow, were *not* generous rebels. They were killers who lived and died by the gun. Still, many law-abiding people identified with bank robbers because the outlaws seemed to act out the struggling person's own resentments of the rich and powerful. Yes, farmers agreed, it is wrong to steal. Yet stealing from those who had "stolen" their own land and homes seemed like simple justice.

"Pretty Boy" Floyd, October 1934.

Son of a depression refugee from Oklahoma takes time out to eat beside a road in California. Photograph taken by Dorothea Lange in 1936.

But many a starving farmer
The same old story told
How the outlaw paid their mortgage
And saved their little homes. . . .

Yes, as through the world I've wandered,
I've seen lots of funny men;
Some will rob with a six-gun,
And some with a fountain pen.

And as through life you travel,
Yes, as through your life you roam,
You won't never see an outlaw
Drive a family from their home.[2]

In 1934, Floyd was shot and killed by a team of FBI agents and local police officers near East Liverpool, Ohio. The funeral, held near his home in Oklahoma, was attended by tens of thousands of people.

The Great Depression was not the only ordeal those living on the Great Plains faced. Farmers, small and large, had stripped the grasslands of its precious cover. Now nature would have its way. For without realizing it, farmers had sown the seeds of a unique tragedy— a tragedy totally beyond their experience. The Dust Bowl.

Dust Bowl Days

*We plowed the prairie and never knew what we were doing,
because we did not know what we were undoing.*

—WENDELL BERRY, FARMER-POET

WHILE THE GREAT DEPRESSION CONTINUED to tighten its grip on America, nature also turned against the suffering nation. Few Americans understood the harm the Great Plow-Up had done to the Great Plains. Nor did the federal government. To those who spent their days behind desks in the nation's capital, it seemed that the fertility of the soil was boundless. Said an official report of the U.S. Department of Agriculture, "The soil is the one . . . resource that cannot be exhausted; that cannot be used up." This statement had more to do with ignorance and wishful thinking than science.[1]

A drought that began in 1930 became the worst in the nation's history, affecting more than three-quarters of the country. Throughout the East, crops withered in the fields and bank foreclosures increased. The next year, the center of the drought shifted westward, to the Great Plains.

As usual, heat went along with drought. Out on the plains, the early 1930s saw record-breaking heat waves. In some states, like Nebraska, the temperature soared to 118 degrees, and stayed there for days without letup or relief. It was so hot that a cook in Grafton, South Dakota, made a melted cheese sandwich by putting it on the sidewalk

PREVIOUS PAGE: A farmer and his sons in a dust storm in Cimarron County, Oklahoma, 1936. The building behind them is probably a farm shed, not their home. RIGHT: "Black Sunday" in Liberal, Kansas, April 14, 1935.

Dust Storm 4-14-35
Turtle Studio, Liberal, Kans.

SOIL DRIFTING OVER HOG HOUSE - S. DAK. - 1935

outside her restaurant. Thousands of people suffered heatstroke, a sudden collapse brought on by extreme heat. Hundreds died. There was no air-conditioning back then, even in town homes with electricity. Residents might have electric fans, but these merely circulated the hot air, so that it felt like a hot hand held over the face. Few farm homes had electricity, and thus most had no electric fans.

The heat was especially severe on the southern plains. In 1934, writer Meridel Le Sueur described how it felt on a sweltering day in Oklahoma:

> . . . it was so hot you couldn't sit around looking at the panting cattle and counting their ribs and listening to that low cry that is an awful asking. We got in a car and drove slowly through the sizzling countryside. Not a soul in sight. It was like a funeral. The houses were closed up tight, the blinds drawn, the windows and doors closed. . . . Through all these windows eyes were watching— watching the wheat go, the rye go, the corn, peas, potatoes go. Everywhere in these barricaded houses were eyes drawn back to the burning windows looking out at . . . food slowly burning in the fields. . . . Then an awful thing happened. The sun went down . . . and men and women began to pour out of the houses, the children lean and fleet as rats, and tired lean farm women looking to see what had happened. The men ran into their fields, ran back for water and they began to water their lands with buckets and cups, running, pouring the puny drops of water on the baked earth as if every minute might count now. . . . Not a word was spoken. In in-

OPPOSITE PAGE: Soil drifting over a hog house in South Dakota in 1935. RIGHT: A snake priest, c. 1900. Some Native Americans believed snakes could carry prayers for rain to the Great Spirit.

The Hopi Snake Dance

"These dances are prayers or invocations for rain, the crowning blessing in this dry land. The rain is adored and invoked both as male and female; the gentle steady downpour is the female, the storm with lightning the male . . . The snakes, the brothers of men, as are all living things in the Hopi creed, are besought to tell the beings of the underworld man's need of water." —Theodore Roosevelt[2]

Hopi snake priest with a snake in his mouth in the Hopi snake dance, c. 1899.

Opposite page: A Dust Bowl farm in the Coldwater District, north of Dalhart, Texas. This house was occupied, though most of the houses in the district were abandoned at the time. Photograph by Dorothea Lange, June 1938.

tense silence they hurried down the rows with buckets and cups, watering the wilted corn plants, a gargantuan and terrible and hopeless labor. . . . Even the children ran with cups of water, all dogged silent, mad, without a word.[3]

In the heat and dryness, billions of grasshoppers hatched from their eggs in the ground. The outbreak was incredible, a plague of biblical scale. Towns turned on their streetlights during the day and lit bonfires on street corners to guide pedestrians. Newspapers reported "cloudbursts of grasshoppers" that, landing, covered everything, ate everything, including sweat-stained rake handles and feathers off turkeys. The voracious insects gnawed the paint off houses, leaving the wood bare. No growing thing escaped their jaws. In Doland, South Dakota, a farmer remembered his father going into a field after the "hoppers" left. The man was crushed. All his hopes, all his hard work, had amounted to—nothing. "He stared at the ground for a long time. It was hard; there wasn't a sprout or root left in it. He started pounding his fists against the ground real hard. His hands were tough, but blood came running out of the knuckles. Then he moaned and started screaming: 'God damn you, land! . . . God damn you, earth!'"[4]

Many plains people turned to religion for support and for rain. The Hopi Indians of Arizona danced their ancient snake dances with rattlesnakes and other native species. Holding the squirming reptiles as they danced, Hopi men caressed them with their hands, kissed them with their lips, then released them to beg the Great Spirit to send rain. White people crowded into churches, singing hymns and praying for an end to the drought. Desperate people turned to su-

perstition. Thinking it might force rain from the sky, some farmers killed snakes and draped them belly-side up along fences; in Kansas, highways were lined for miles by dead snakes on barbed wire, their bellies facing skyward. Elsewhere, farmers hired traveling rainmakers to explode dynamite in balloons floating high above the earth's surface. The idea was to "agitate" the atmosphere, causing clouds to form and rain to fall. Farmers would have done better to save their money. For instead of the rain, the winds came, and with them the dust.

As mentioned, periodic dust storms are normal on the Great Plains. People expected them. Since nothing could be done about the storms, you accepted the inconvenience and waited until they passed. Yet the dust storms of the 1930s were different. They were not "natural disasters," like hurricanes, tornadoes, and earthquakes, over which humans have no control. Humans can neither make such natural disasters, nor prevent them. Although dust storms would have occurred anyhow, human actions made the storms of the 1930s much worse than they would have been. The result was an ecological catastrophe.

This catastrophe has a simple explanation. A Texas sheepherder explained a basic fact: "Grass is what counts. It's what saves us all— far as we get saved. . . . Grass is what holds the earth together."[5] Plowing up millions of acres of drought-resistant native grasses removed the very thing that had held plains soil in place for countless centuries. Replacing these grasses with cash crops like wheat and corn added to the problem. Unlike native grasses, which continue to grow year after year, these crops are annuals; that is, they die after

The Black Sunday dust storm in Baca County, Colorado, Easter Sunday 1935.

a single growing season. Because the crops live for only one season and have shallow root systems, they do not survive prolonged heat and dry spells.

Thus, all the elements for disaster came together in the 1930s: drought, heat, sod-destroying farming methods, annual cash crops. When the winds came, the ground cracked and the dust became airborne. And so, the dust-storm catastrophe of the 1930s was no natural disaster. It was manmade.

For people already reeling under the hardships of the Great Depression, life in the Dust Bowl became the supreme test of the human spirit. What was it like for them?

Mammoth dust storms gave the era its nickname, the "dirty thirties." The storms began in 1933, on the northern plains. At first, they were not particularly alarming. Plains people were used to dust storms and expected them to end quickly. Instead, the storms grew in number, lasted longer, and were more severe than any in living memory.

A farmer described the 1934 dust storms as "lollapaloosas," slang for unimaginably large. On May 9, cool Canadian winds whipped up an immense dust cloud over Montana and Wyoming. Government scientists estimated that this storm alone carried away 350 million tons of topsoil. For the next two days, dust clouds raced south and east. Airline pilots climbed up to fifteen thousand feet to reach clear air; the dust would have clogged their engines, causing them to burn out. Some 12 million tons of dust enveloped Chicago in a gritty haze—four pounds for every man, woman, and child in the Windy City. On May 12, the *New York Times* reported, "a cloud of dust thousands of feet high . . . filtered the rays of the sun for five hours yesterday. New York was obscured in a half-light similar to the light cast by the sun

Electrical Storms

Trillions of dust particles striking against each other generated static electricity. Sometimes there was so much electricity in the air that it knocked people down if they shook hands. Static electricity made the barbs on barbed wire fences glow. Animals blown into wire fences could be seriously injured by the electrical charge. To avoid shocks, housewives covered door handles with cloth. Motorists had to outfit cars with chains to drag for grounding, or risk having their engines short out in a storm.[6]

A dust storm overtakes automobiles and a group of houses on the Colorado plains.

OPPOSITE PAGE: An approaching dust storm in Prowers County, Colorado, March 1937.

in a partial eclipse." Three hundred miles out at sea, sailors wrote their names in the dust that settled on ships' decks.

The storm that farmers call "the granddaddy of 'em all" burst out of South Dakota on April 14, 1935—"Black Sunday." Gathering force while growing in size, this monster was over one thousand miles wide. It traveled fifteen hundred miles before breaking up over the Gulf of Mexico. People who saw the cloud from different angles said it ranged from two miles to only several hundred feet in height. Young children did not know what to make of it. In the town of Guymon in the Oklahoma Panhandle, a little girl turned to her father and said, "Oh, look here, God's coming!" Her father replied, "It looks more like hell to me."[7]

In nearby Pampa, Texas, the day began gloriously. The air was so clear you could see to the horizon in all directions. Texan A. D. Kirk had just parked his car when he saw something strange.

> I noticed a low dark line of what I first thought was a cloud along the northern horizon. It made no sense. There was not a cloud in the sky. As I watched, it got taller and spread from the west to the east horizon. The black mass was coming on fast. . . . The front of the cloud was a rolling, tumbling, boiling mass of dust and dirt about two hundred feet high, almost vertical, and as black as an Angus bull. There was no dust in the air above it or in front of it. It came across the prairie like a two-hundred-foot-high tidal wave, pushed along by a sixty-mile-per-hour wind. When it got to a house or power pole or any other object, the house or whatever disappeared. It was weird. After the front passed, the

Street view of a dust storm in Scott City, Kansas, 1935.

For Want of Oxygen

When a dust storm struck, family members quickly sealed windows and doors with gummed tape, felt strips, or rags. This cut air circulation to such a degree that lamps flickered for lack of oxygen and breathing became difficult. When someone felt as if they might pass out, a window was opened just a bit, letting in a swirling dust-deluge. Yet even with every opening sealed, the dust, fine as talcum powder, got in through invisible cracks.

The kitchen of a house in Williams County, North Dakota, 1937. Notice the windowpane stuffed with rags in a vain attempt to keep the dust out.

darkness rivaled the darkness inside a whale resting on the bottom of the ocean at midnight. . . .[8]

While many thought Black Sunday heralded doomsday, others saw a chance to make a fast profit. Collecting dust in old soda bottles, they offered it for sale as "Genuine 1935 Rolling Duster Dust—25 cents."[9] Sales could not have been very good. Most who had lived through Black Sunday wanted to forget it. But nature would not let them forget.

Although nothing equaled the Black Sunday blizzard of 1935, for the next four years scores of dust storms swept across the Great Plains. While different places fared better or worse in any given year, the true Dust Bowl, the hardest-hit region, centered in the five states of the southern plains. This region, stretching roughly five hundred miles by three hundred miles, included the western third of Kansas, southeastern Colorado, the Oklahoma Panhandle, the northern two-thirds of the Texas Panhandle, and northeastern New Mexico. "If you would like to have your heart broken, just come out here," wrote Ernie Pyle, among the era's finest reporters. "This is the dust-storm country. It is the saddest land I have ever seen."[10]

Dust storms usually came on suddenly, as A. D. Kirk noted. When one developed, people could, at the very best, hope for a radio report as it passed over a neighboring state or county. Without that, you knew a dust storm was on its way when the wind picked up and you saw the dark clouds boiling over the horizon. Even today, with computers and other high-tech equipment, it is impossible to predict when a dust storm will develop or what course it will take. It is easier to predict the course of a hurricane and where it is most likely to strike.

Dust is too much for a farmer's son in Cimarron
County, Oklahoma, April 1936.

As dust clouds appeared, people rushed to bring their children home from school. If the storm moved too quickly and their parents could not get there in time, the children stayed in the school building. Teachers lit oil lamps while the children slept at their desks or lay on the bare floor. Hopefully, the school had some food and water on hand; if not, everyone went hungry for the duration of the storm. Nobody went outside until it passed, for fear of getting lost and suffocating.

Meanwhile, families hunkered down at home. A woman in Garden City, Kansas, told how it felt to sit helplessly while sheets of wind-blown dust lashed her house.

> All we could do about it was just sit in our dusty chairs, gaze at each other through the fog that filled the room and watch the fog settle slowly and silently, covering everything—including ourselves—in a thick, brownish gray blanket. . . . The door and windows were all shut tightly, yet those tiny particles seemed to seep through the very walls. It got into cupboards and clothes closets; our faces were as dirty as if we had rolled in the dirt; our hair was gray and stiff and we ground dirt between our teeth.[11]

Sleeping became a challenge. Families lay in bed on wet sheets, hoping to get some relief from the stifling heat. Many slept with damp rags over their faces, and even stuffed Vaseline in their nostrils to prevent breathing in the dust while the storm lasted or until the dust settled after it had passed. In some places, the Red Cross handed out gas masks, leftovers from the First World War, to keep children from suffocating in their sleep. Although designed to keep out poison gas, masks sometimes let in microscopic dust particles. "We try to lie still," a man said, "because every turn stirs the dust on the blankets.

After a while, if we are good sleepers, we forget." Upon waking, everything had a coating of dust. Sheets, now stiff with mud, often had the imprint of those who had slept on them.

Dust Bowl people fought a never-ending battle for cleanliness. After a storm, families attacked the dust in their homes with brooms, scoops, shovels, and buckets. Women flapped wet towels to collect powdery dust that hung in the air. Sometimes they cleared the air with water from a handheld spray gun normally used for liquid insect repellant. The only problem was that dust particles caught in droplets of water covered the walls and floor in mud.

In her *Dust Bowl Diary*, Ann Marie Low, a North Dakota rancher's daughter, told of cleaning up after a black blizzard. For four solid days, Ann Marie's life was nothing but wash, wash, wash.

The mess was incredible! Dirt had blown into the house all week and lay inches deep on everything. Every towel and curtain was just black. There wasn't a clean dish or cooking utensil. . . . It took until 10 o'clock to wash all the dirty dishes. That's not wiping them—just washing them. The cupboards had to be washed out to have a clean place to put them. . . . Every room had to have dirt almost shoveled out of it before we could wash floors and furniture. . . . Every towel, curtain, piece of bedding, and every garment had to be taken outdoors to have as much dust as possible shaken out before washing. The cistern is dry, so I had to carry all the water needed from the well. . . . Life in what the newspapers call 'the Dust Bowl' is becoming a gritty nightmare.[14]

68

The Black Sunday dust storm in Rolla, Kansas. A friend sent this photo to President Roosevelt on May 16, 1935, with the following inscription: "Dear Mr. Roosevelt, Darkness came when it hit us. Picture taken from water tower one hundred feet high. Yours Truly, Chas. P. Williams."

A rolling dust storm approaches Elkhart, Kansas, in May, 1937. As seen from Main Street at about 3:00 P.M.

Opposite page: Son of a farmer in the dust of Cimarron County, Oklahoma. April, 1936.

Before serving meals, farm women set their tables with plates, cups, and glasses turned upside down to keep them clean. Water and milk were kept in tightly sealed jars. Food was cooked at high temperature so the rising current of hot air lifted the dust away from the food. Sometimes the cooking was done under open umbrellas. Meals had to be eaten quickly.

Transportation all but came to a halt during black blizzards. The blowing dust drifted like snow; in places, nine-foot sand drifts buried roads, signs, and landmarks. Sand dunes larger than those at a beach formed. With no grass to anchor them, the wind made drifts and dunes "migrate." They rolled across the land like tidal waves, covering all in their paths. Trains ground to a stop. Driving a car in a dust cloud was dangerous. With visibility nearly zero, headlights were practically useless. Newspaper reporter Lorena Hickok, a friend of First Lady Eleanor Roosevelt's, wrote:

We had gone less than ten miles when we had to turn back. It kept getting worse. You couldn't see a foot ahead of the car. It was a truly terrifying experience. Like driving in a fog, only worse because of the wind that seemed as if it would blow the car right off the road. It was as though we were picked up in a vast, impenetrable black cloud which was hurling us right off the earth.[15]

Luckily, Ms. Hickok turned back in time. Other drivers, blinded by swirling dust, skidded into ditches or crashed into oncoming vehicles. Local newspapers grimly announced dust-related auto deaths.

Being caught outdoors on foot during a dust storm meant trouble. At the very least, high winds picked up spiny thistles and drove them

Men try to get a car to move through dust accumulated on the road. Photo was taken about eight miles southwest of Felt, Oklahoma, in Cimarron County in February, 1939.

into people's faces, so that even little children resembled whiskered old men. Windblown dust acted as sandpaper, scraping paint off cars, shredding crops, and rubbing skin off faces.

Many people who got lost on foot in the blinding dust died, or nearly died, within a few feet of safety. Glenn D. McMurry, a Kansas farmer, went out one evening during a lull in a dust storm.

> **I went to the shed to milk one of our cows. Before I had finished, the wind came up and the dust became so dense that I could barely see. I finished milking and headed for [my] house. The wind was blowing hard by this time and one's voice could barely be heard above it. After walking for a while, I realized I was in danger of . . . wandering aimlessly in the fields. With my hand outstretched I proceeded to walk in what I hoped was the right direction. Suddenly, I felt something and I realized it was the corner of the house. As a matter of fact, had I been a few inches further to my right, I would have missed it entirely. I have shuddered many times since. What if I had missed the house! After that incident, I stretched a wire between the house and the milk shed to help me find my way back should another storm overtake me as this one had.[16]**

McMurry had a close call, but survived. Others did not. A seven-year-old Oklahoma boy wandered away from home during a dust storm; his parents found him hours later, suffocated. Another time, two children left school together, only to get caught in a sudden dust storm. They wandered around for hours before dropping from exhaustion; the next day, searchers found their bodies half-buried in dust.[17]

Inhaling dust had long-lasting effects. After a storm, a survivor recalled, "people spat up clods of dirt, sometimes three to four inches long and as big around as a pencil." Many fell ill with silicosis, a lung disease caused by inhaling dust from various minerals or coal. Miners called the disease "black lung," plains people "dust pneumonia." By whatever name, the dust acted like powdered glass, slowly cutting the lungs to shreds. The outlook for sufferers was poor, as folksinger Woody Guthrie says in one of his Dust Bowl Ballads.

> *I got that dust new-mon-ee, new-mon-ee in my lungs*
> *And I'm gonna sing that dust new-mon-ee song.*
> *I went to the doctor and the doctor said, "My son*
> *You got the dust new-mon-ee, an' you aint got long, not long."*
> *Now there ought to be some yodelin' in this song*
> *But I can't yodel for the rattlin' in my lungs.*[18]

Dust pneumonia victims generally died in pain and gasping for breath, just like poison-gas victims. Moreover, people with asthma died at higher rates in the Dust Bowl region than elsewhere in the country. So did the elderly and newborns.

Animals suffered dreadfully during dust storms. Caroline Henderson sympathized with the poor creatures. She and her husband, Will, were farmers in the Oklahoma Panhandle. Also a talented writer, Caroline's articles on farm life in the Dust Bowl years appeared in the *Atlantic Monthly* magazine. One day, she found a jackrabbit trembling with fear outside her kitchen door. A dust storm had blown out one of its eyes, so she fed it and put it in with her pet guinea pigs. That experience made Caroline wonder what the future held for plains farmers. She wrote: "When these wild creatures, ordinarily so

Animals Suffered Dreadfully

In a black blizzard, streams could fill with mud, suffocating all the fish. Birds overtaken by dust clouds lost their bearings and slammed into buildings, grain silos, and telephone poles. "In Texas," said one observer, "the windswept hayfields were alive with blinded sparrows."[19] Dust blew into the eyes of cattle. Mixing with tears, it turned to mud, which hardened and cemented their eyelids shut. Blinded, the cattle wandered until they collapsed from exhaustion. Then the sand covered them as the blizzards of the Big Die-Up had covered cattle forty years earlier. Even if a farmer could afford cattle feed, the sand in it scraped the animals' teeth away. Unable to chew, they starved.

Cattle graze fruitlessly in a cornfield ruined by drought and grasshoppers. Photograph taken near Carson, North Dakota, in July 1936.

Drought farmers in Sallisaw, Oklahoma, line the shady side of the main street in town while their crops burn up in the fields. Photograph by Dorothea Lange, August 1936.

well able to take care of themselves, come seeking protection, their necessity indicates a cruel crisis for man and beast."[20]

The dust storms were more than a cruel physical ordeal. Mentally, they affected people in various ways. Storms might strike days, or weeks, apart. You never knew when, so people on the plains lived in a constant state of anxiety. Some became short-tempered, shouting at loved ones for any reason, or no reason at all. Unable to take the strain, a few lost their minds and wound up in insane asylums. Now and then, people (usually men) committed suicide, even shot their families, saying "we're all better off dead."[21]

But in the worst of times, most Dust Bowl people tried to keep their sense of humor. It was a way of preserving their sanity, of keeping their spirits up by joking about their troubles.

People told tall tales about birds flying backward to keep the dust out of their eyes, and dust so thick that prairie dogs burrowed ten feet in the air. "I hope it'll rain before the kids grow up," a farmer said. "They ain't never seen none before." You knew a dust storm was coming when sidewinders (rattlesnakes) began to sneeze. Then there was the pilot who parachuted from his plane in a dust storm, only to take six hours to shovel his way to the ground. Jokesters told of the farmer who went to a banker for a loan, only to see his land blowing past the window.[22]

Jokes aside, the people of the Dust Bowl faced grim choices. How could they make a living in this dangerous new wasteland? Should they stay where they were, hoping things would get better, or leave? If they left, where would they go?

'Cross the mountains to the sea,
Come the wife and kids and me.
It's a hot and dusty highway
For a dust bowl refugee. . . .

I'm a dust bowl refugee,
I'm a dust bowl refugee,
And I wonder will I always
Be a dust bowl refugee?

— WOODY GUTHRIE, **DUST BOWL REFUGEES**, 1938

AMERICANS DURING THE GREAT DEPRESSION were on the move. People unable to make a living at home decided to search for work elsewhere. If they had a few dollars to spare, they bought a train or bus ticket to a place they thought might need workers. If they were broke, they hitchhiked or rode in railroad boxcars. Known as hobos, they were usually ordinary folks—some just children—who wandered about and lived by begging and doing odd jobs.

One boy wanderer, Eric Sevareid, recalled that leaving home was like entering an alien world.

[It was] the great underground world, peopled by tens of thousands of American men, women, and children, white, black, brown, and yellow, who inhabit the "jungle," eat from blackened tin cans, find warmth at night in the boxcars, take the sun by day

PREVIOUS PAGE: "Laundry facilities" in a migratory labor camp in Imperial Valley, California, near Calipatria. Photograph by Dorothea Lange in the spring of 1937. RIGHT: Boys hopping freight. A very dangerous, even deadly, way for those with no money for train fare to travel in search of work.

On the Road, On the Rails

"Hoboing" was dangerous. In trying to "hop a freight"—climb onto a moving freight train—one could easily fall under the wheels. Yet, with no opportunities at home, many were willing to take such risks. Approximately 250,000 boys and girls, some as young as nine, became hobos in the 1930s. One young hobo, Eric Sevareid, eventually found success as a broadcast journalist. During World War II he became famous for his live reports of the German air raids of London, given by radio as the bombs fell.

Eric Sevareid in 1947

on the flat cars, steal one day, beg with cap in hand the next, fight with fists and often razors . . . wander from town to town, anxious for the next place, tired of it in a day, fretting to be gone again, happy only when the wheels are clicking under them, the telephone poles slipping by.[1]

While hobos traveled singly or with a group of friends, others left home as families, by automobile. These were the "tin-can tourists," the refugees from the Dust Bowl. The effects of economic depression and dust storms spread through farm communities like contagious diseases. Towns that depended on farmers for their livelihood withered away as their customers went broke. Unable to collect local taxes, towns cut or eliminated public services: schools, hospitals, even police. Boarded-up shops lined main streets. Falling contributions forced churches to close their doors. Tumbleweeds blew through towns across the southern plains.

In a way, history was repeating itself. It was an old story, one that started with European immigration to America. Needy people always had to decide whether to hang on at home, hoping for better days, or to pull up stakes and begin anew elsewhere. It was the same with inhabitants of the Dust Bowl. Most decided to hang on; three out of four stayed put, making ends meet as best they could. Kansan Aida Buell Norris explained why:

Why do we stay? In part because we hope for the coming of moisture, which would change conditions so we can again have bountiful harvests. And in great part, because it is home. We have

Drought refugees from Oklahoma looking for work in the pea fields of California. Photograph taken near San José Mission by Dorothea Lange.

Working Well and Cheap

For generations, migrant workers from Mexico had crossed the U.S. border illegally to harvest the Golden State's fruit and vegetable crops. Growers welcomed them because they worked well and cheaply. Yet the Depression changed all that. To protect jobs for unemployed American citizens, Congress passed harsh laws against illegal immigrants, forcing most Mexicans to return to their homeland. To replace them, growers sent thousands of leaflets to the Dust Bowl states. "PLENTY OF WORK!" said the leaflets in bold type. "GOOD WAGES!" "GOOD HOUSES!" "COME TO SUNNY CALIFORNIA!" It sounded too good to be true—and it was.

An Hispanic cotton picker in Southern San Joaquin Valley, California, November 1936. Photograph by Dorothea Lange.

reared our family here and many have precious memories of the past. We have our memories. We have faith in the future, we are here to stay.[2]

Those who decided to leave did so out of a combination of need and hope. Farm folk were tough-minded, proud people used to making their own way in the world. For those who had been "blown-out" of their farms by black blizzards, or lost their land to banks because they could not make mortgage payments, leaving sometimes seemed their best bet. Yet they were also optimistic about the future. Dust Bowl refugees did not see themselves as paupers, but as "regular folks" who had fallen on bad luck. They hoped to find work elsewhere, save money, buy some farmland, and start over. Many just abandoned their old homes. As Woody Guthrie put it in his song, "The Great Dust Storm":

We loaded our jalopies and piled our families in,
We rattled down that highway to never come back again.[3]

In the five years after Black Sunday, 1935, no fewer than 2.5 million people left their homes on the Great Plains. It is often claimed to be the largest migration in American history. Most did not go very far, perhaps to the next county or to a town, where they just managed to scrape by. Another 300,000 headed toward where the sun set, to California.

The main road west was no longer a dirt wagon trail but Route 66. You cannot find this road on most of today's maps. Modern interstate

Once Missouri farmers, now migratory farm laborers on the California coast. Their eyes tell the story of what they have gone through. Photo by Dorothea Lange, February 1936.

highways have replaced it. Yet "Old 66" was once the best-known highway in the country. A double ribbon of concrete stretching roughly twenty-four-hundred miles, it crossed eight states. Unlike most American highways, it did not follow a straight line. A road of "hooks, elbows, and hairpin turns," it linked a dozen cities and hundreds of small towns between Chicago, Illinois, and Santa Monica, California.

With luck, and no breakdowns, a trip of three or four days lay ahead of each family. A car could make it to California for about ten dollars worth of gasoline, no small sum for those who had to watch every penny. (What cost $10 in 1935 cost $138 in 2005).

In his award-winning novel, *The Grapes of Wrath*, John Steinbeck described what the trip was like. Every day cars streamed westward along Route 66. Steinbeck called it "the mother road, the road of flight." That was a good name.[4]

They drove steadily, stopping only to relieve themselves by the roadside, eat a quick meal, and allow their car's radiator to cool. Now and then, they stopped at a filling station for gasoline and oil. At night, if they decided to splurge, they slept in a cheap motor court, an early version of the motel. Usually, however, they tried to camp behind a billboard, which would shade them from the morning sun.

OPPOSITE PAGE: Vernon Evans of Lemmon, South Dakota, near Missoula, Montana, on Highway 10. July, 1936. Leaving a grasshopper-ridden and drought-stricken area for a new start in Oregon or Washington, he and his family make about two hundred miles a day in their Model T Ford.
RIGHT: Drought refugees from Abilene, Texas, following the crops of California as migratory workers. "The finest people in this world live in Texas but I just can't seem to accomplish nothin' there. Two year drought, then a crop, then two years drought and so on. I got two brothers still trying to make it back there and there they're sitting," said the father. Photo by Dorothea Lange, August 1936.

See How They Run

The cars looked pretty much alike. Rattling and wheezing, coated with dust, the aging vehicles swayed under loads they were not designed to bear. Inside and outside, tied to the trunk, roof, and running boards, were all the family's worldly possessions. There were bedsprings and bedding; tools; groceries; pots, pans, dishes, and silverware; baskets, bottles, basins, and buckets; washtubs and washboards. Now and then, a goat or chickens rode in a cage tied to a running board. Passengers scarcely had space for themselves.

No School Today

Schooling for Dust Bowl children was a problem whether families decided to stay on their farms or take to the road. Migrant children were not welcomed into schools where the displaced stopped and camped. Instead of going to school, children often worked alongside their parents to bring whatever money they could into the family. In some migrant camps, organizers did arrange nursery schools to look after young children while their parents went into the fields to work.

Education wasn't much easier to find for those that stayed put. Ike Olsteen's family lived on the high plains of Colorado. During the Dust Bowl years, he recalls, one day a boy would be sitting next to him in school, same as always, and the next day the seat would be empty, the boy gone for good.

Storms made travel dangerous and the dusty air was unhealthy to breathe even on calm days. The Red Cross advised everyone in the region, but particularly children and the elderly, to stay inside as much as possible. Of the nine children in the Olsteen family, only one, Ike, stayed with books till his senior year. With so few children in attendance, many schools closed. In 1935, the state of Kansas alone made plans to close four hundred schools.[8]

"Each member," said Steinbeck, "had his duty and went to it without instruction: children to gather wood, to carry water; men to pitch the tents and bring down the beds; women to cook the supper and to watch while the family fed."[5]

On they drove, across Oklahoma, Texas, New Mexico, and Arizona. In western Arizona, at a flyspeck of a town called Needles, they crossed the Colorado River into California's Mojave Desert. Before entering this 143-mile-long oven, they saw warning signs, like the one that hung from a tall cholla cactus: "CARRY WATER OR THIS IS WHAT YOU'LL LOOK LIKE."

It was best to cross the desert at night, and move slowly, so as not to overheat the car's engine. The Mojave was no place to break down. If, God forbid, you did, people were instructed never to stray from their car, but wait for another car to come, however long that might take. The desert had no mercy. Anyone who wandered into it, even a short distance, was bound to get lost and die of exposure. There were no air-conditioned cars back then, so those crossing in daylight wrapped damp towels around their heads. The windows stayed open, sending a hot breeze through the car.[6]

At last, the refugees reached Barstow, then turned off Route 66, onto California Highway 58. Ahead lay the San Joaquin Valley, among the most fertile spots on earth. "It was paradise," Trice Masters, then a child, recalled years later. "When we saw the valley we started hollerin' and yellin' 'cause we knew it was Californ."[7]

"Californ" was *not* paradise. Many Californians saw Dust Bowl refugees not as fellow Americans, but as rivals for scarce city jobs.

OPPOSITE PAGE: Migrant children sitting in the backseat of the family car in Muskogee County, Oklahoma. June, 1939.

Besides, the plains people seemed so odd, so different—so alien. Travel-stained and wearing frayed clothes, they spoke with a grating Western twang.

Native Californians called the newcomers Okies, because many of them came from Oklahoma. Yet Okie signified more than a place of origin. The term, Woody Guthrie explained, "means you ain't got no home. Sort of meant, too, that you're out of a job. Or owe more than you can rake or scrape [up]." More Dust Bowl refugees came from other plains states than from Oklahoma. No matter. Californians lumped them together as Okies. The name stuck. While others used it as an insult, Okies felt they had nothing to be ashamed of, or to apologize for. To them, the term was another word for stick-to-itiveness, grit, and courage in the face of incredible hardship.[9]

Large corporations controlled California agriculture. Factory farms grew more than two hundred crops for markets in the United States and abroad. The crops included peaches, plums, grapes, nuts, lemons, oranges, lettuce, asparagus, tomatoes, and cotton. All had to be picked by hand, then boxed, bailed, or bagged for shipment.

Growers wanted to keep workers' wages low and their own profits high. So, the leaflets they distributed in the Dust Bowl states were meant to encourage more people to come to California than there were jobs. John Steinbeck had a character in *The Grapes of Wrath* describe a typical hiring scene:

OPPOSITE PAGE: Family walking on highway with five children. They started in Idabel, Oklahoma, and were bound for Krebs, Oklahoma. The father was taken sick with pneumonia and lost the farm. Photograph by Dorothea Lange, June 1938. RIGHT: Children of Oklahoma drought refugees on a highway near Bakersfield, California. This family of six had no shelter, no food, no money, and almost no gasoline. The child had bone tuberculosis. Photograph by Dorothea Lange, June 1935.

The Bum Blockade

Many of the "decent" people of California wanted no part of the down-and-out Dust Bowl refugees. For a few weeks, Los Angeles police chief James E. Davis set up an illegal "bum blockade" along the Arizona border to keep the Okies out. But the courts ruled the blockade illegal, for Americans have the right to travel anywhere in their own country.

Tom Collins, manager of Kern migrant camp in California, with a drought refugee family, November 1936. Photograph by Dorothea Lange.

OPPOSITE PAGE: A family from Dallas on the way to the Arkansas Delta, where they hoped to find work in the cotton fields, August 1936. They had no money or food for the journey. The father had stopped to repair a tire. As he told photographer Dorothea Lange, "It's tough but life's tough anyway you take it."

Maybe he [the grower] needs two hundred men, so he talks to five hundred, an' they tell other folks, an' when you get to the place, they's a thousan' men. This here fella says, "I'm payin' twenty cents an hour." An' maybe half a the men walk off. But they's still five hundred that's so goddamn hungry they'll work for nothin' but biscuits. . . . You see now? The more fellas he can get, less he's gonna pay. An' he'll get a fella with kids if he can.[10]

Hired hands lived on their employer's farm during the planting and harvest seasons. The workers' quarters, not much more than tar-paper shacks, were without electricity or running water. The little money migrants earned went for food in the company store, which charged higher prices than a market in a distant town. Many went into debt at the company store, becoming what they called "wage slaves." That is, while they owed the grower money, they had to take whatever wages he offered to cancel their debt. Yet these were the "lucky" ones. At least they could feed their children—sort of.

Children also worked in the fields. One day, reporter John L. Spivak visited a California cotton farm. Here is what he found:

When I walked out in the field there was this little girl dragging a huge sack along a furrow, and stuffing the cotton bolls into it. She looked so tired, so weary. . . . "How old are you?" I asked.

She looked up and smiled pleasantly. "Fifteen."

"Working in the fields long?"

"Uh-uh."

"How old were you when you started?"

She shrugged her shoulders. "Dunno. Maybe eight. Maybe nine. I dunno."[11]

Jobless migrants, homeless, their last pennies gone, gathered in "ditch camps." As the name suggests, these camps were pitched along roadside drainage ditches or irrigation ditches leading into the fields. For fifty years, reformers had crusaded against city slums, dreadful places where large families lived in one or two cubbyhole-sized rooms, amid filth and disease. These slums were almost comfortable compared to ditch camps. In one, social workers found a family of ten living in a broken-down Ford. "The mother . . . was trying to carry on a homelife as best she could, using cupboards and tables made of old boxes, a rusty tin can as her stewpot, wash water taken out of an irrigation ditch, the side of which served as their toilet."[12]

Having escaped the dust storms, the refugees faced the horrors of crowding, poor diet, filth, and polluted water. Epidemics of typhoid fever, pneumonia, and tuberculosis swept through the ditch camps. In some camps, social workers reported children dying at the rate of two a day, and "dozens of children with horribly sore eyes . . . fever, colds, and sore throats." They also found many cases of illnesses caused by waterborne bacteria: stomach cramps, diarrhea, and dysentery—uncontrollable diarrhea mixed with blood and mucus. Unable to retain water in their bodies, dysentery victims died of dehydration.[13]

What could be done to relieve such misery, and by whom? This was the big question that faced the American people during the "dirty

Oklahoma squatter family in Riverside County, California, in 1935. Photograph by Dorothea Lange.

OPPOSITE PAGE: A squatter camp in California, November 1936. Photograph by Dorothea Lange.

Part of an impoverished family of nine on a New Mexico highway, August 1936. They were depression refugees from Iowa. The father, an auto mechanic and a painter, was ill with tuberculosis. The family was about to sell their belongings and trailer for money to buy food. "We don't want to go where we'll be a nuisance to anybody," they said. Photograph by Dorothea Lange.

thirties." For the nation to survive, many believed the federal government, and the American people, had to battle the Great Depression and the Dust Bowl in any way they could. As Franklin D. Roosevelt proclaimed in his 1932 campaign for the presidency:

The millions who are in want will not stand by silently forever while the things to satisfy their needs are within easy reach. We need enthusiasm, imagination and the ability to face facts, even unpleasant ones, bravely. We need to correct, by drastic means if necessary, the faults in our economic system from which we now suffer. We need the courage of the young. Yours is not the task of making your way in the world, but the task of remaking the world which you will find before you. May every one of us be granted the courage, the faith and the vision to give the best that is in us to that remaking!

The New Deal

I see one-third of a nation ill-housed, ill-clad, ill-nourished. The test of our progress is not whether we add more to the abundance of those who have much; it is whether we provide enough for those who have too little.

—PRESIDENT FRANKLIN D. ROOSEVELT, 1937

IN 1932, VOTERS ELECTED FRANKLIN D. Roosevelt president in a landslide victory. "FDR," as everyone called him, was a wealthy New Yorker who had been stricken with polio a decade earlier. Paralyzed from the waist down, his legs useless, FDR knew about suffering firsthand. Through suffering, he grew as a person, developing deep sympathy for the downtrodden. That, in turn, shaped his ideas about government. Roosevelt believed that government was the people's servant, not its master. In times of trouble, he insisted, the chief duty of the federal government was to help those who could no longer help themselves.

Roosevelt called his program to fight the Great Depression the New Deal. At the president's urging, Congress passed hundreds of reform measures, which he then signed into law. For example, the Banking Act insured bank deposits and prevented banks from investing in risky ventures. The Social Security Act guaranteed pensions for elderly people, who might otherwise spend their last years in poverty. The Works Projects (changed to Progress in 1939) Administration

PREVIOUS PAGE: A woman welder at a California plant during World War II. She works on a part of the exhaust system for a Valiant basic trainer, widely used to train Air Force pilots.

RIGHT: Franklin D. Roosevelt in 1931, as governor of New York State.

created jobs for the unemployed, building roads, bridges, and other public works. The Civilian Conservation Corps gave young men (but not young women) jobs planting trees, fighting forest fires, building wilderness roads, and creating wildlife refuges.

New Deal measures were also aimed at helping refugees from the Dust Bowl. In 1936, the Farm Security Administration, a branch of the Department of Agriculture, built thirteen migrant camps in California. While these were not nearly enough, given the number of migrants, such emergency shelters relieved a great deal of suffering. The agency built its first camp, called Weedpatch, just south of the city of Bakersfield in the San Joaquin Valley. Used as a model for the others, Weedpatch provided clean water, showers, toilets, and food. Migrants lived in canvas tents and one-room cabins. Led by camp administrators, they formed self-governing committees to clean the camps, exchange job information, and generally see that things ran smoothly.

Back in the Dust Bowl states, the federal government developed plans to help those farmers, the majority, who had not joined the exodus. At Roosevelt's urging, the Farm Security Administration offered farmers low-interest loans, emergency supplies, and livestock feed.

Another federal agency, the Agricultural Adjustment Administration—AAA for short—attacked the problem of low prices for farm products. It followed that, if prices fell because production was too high, lowering production would raise farm incomes. Thus, AAA paid farmers to cultivate less land and destroy existing crops. Dur-

Okies Have Lice

Surrounding communities resented the newcomers. Some locals assumed that, because Okies were poor, they deserved to be poor—had brought poverty upon themselves through laziness, ignorance, and "immorality." Too often, Okie children met bias in school. "The better dressed children shout and jeer," a parent told John Steinbeck. "The teachers are quite often impatient with these additions to their duties, and the parents of the 'nice' children do not want to have disease carriers in their schools." After all, everyone just "knew" that "Okies have lice."[1]

A Champion for the Soil

"Of all the countries of the world," Hugh Bennett said, "we Americans have been the greatest destroyers of land of any race of people barbaric or civilized." Americans changed the land more than "the combined activities of volcanoes, earthquakes, tidal waves, tornadoes and all the excavations of mankind since the beginning of history."[3] Bennett became the first chief of the Soil Conservation Service.

"Big Hugh," the son of a North Carolina cotton planter, was a graduate of the University of North Carolina specializing in soil science. He once asked an unwilling congressional committee to expand the soil conservation program. As he spoke, a cloud of plains dust enveloped Washington. "This, gentleman," he said, "is what I have been talking about." The committee approved his request.

Hugh Hammond Bennett (right), inspecting seedlings.

ing AAA's first year, 1933, farmers plowed under millions of acres of wheat, corn, and cotton. Livestock breeders killed six million baby pigs and two hundred thousand sows. Economists called this "planned scarcity." While farmers, and not just those on the plains, benefited from rising prices, Roosevelt's critics protested. They thought it "utterly idiotic" that consumers, especially the jobless, should pay more for food. Wealthy farmers even *increased* production. While taking their poorer-quality land out of cultivation, they used their government checks to buy more tractors and combines to cultivate their best lands more efficiently.[2] Although their actions challenged the idea of "planned scarcity," at least these farmers lowered food prices for the needy.

The rain-starved plains posed special problems. Farmers there suffered not only from the Great Depression, but also from their lands literally blowing away. Luckily, Roosevelt had a top-notch adviser. Hugh Hammond Bennett was a high official in the Department of Agriculture and an expert in soil science. Fear that America was losing its fertile soil through erosion and wasteful farming methods made him a champion of soil conservation. Eventually known as "the father of soil conservation," Bennett was ahead of his time. For years, he had warned about the dangers of sodbusting and destroying native grasses.

Through "Big Hugh," the president learned the basics of soil science. Roosevelt came to realize that the Dust Bowl was not the result of bad weather and bad luck. It was an avoidable disaster. The villain, Bennett kept insisting, was human ignorance and, yes, greed, which led to abuse of the land.

Bennett and his agronomists, experts in managing the soil and improving crop production, wanted to improve conditions during their own time while also acting to avert future Dust Bowls. Before going ahead with their plans, however, they first had to get public opinion on their side. That was no easy task, for their plans would cost taxpayers money when money was scarce. Moreover, plains people were set in their ways. They did not take to change easily, or think much of "experts" from Washington telling them how to farm. Hoping to overcome resistance, the Farm Security Administration hired moviemakers and photographers to gather evidence illustrating the need for change. These efforts brought two talented artists instant fame.

Pare Lorentz, a thirty-year-old movie critic, had never made a film himself. Now he got his chance. Working under a Farm Security Administration contract, in 1936 Lorentz released his first documentary film, *The Plow that Broke the Plains.* Using dramatic footage, Lorentz showed how farmers had ravaged the Texas Panhandle. Viewers saw lines of tractors advancing across virgin grasslands to the sound of military marches, like tank columns through Europe during the First World War. Easterners could almost smell and breathe the clouds of windborne dust blowing off the southern plains. The film's message, driven home with all the delicacy of a baseball bat, was clear. The plains would only support people if they respected the land and lived in harmony with it.

Dorothea Lange focused on people rather than on the land. A rarity at a time when nearly all professional photographers were men, she was a well-known portrait photographer with her own studio in San

This poster for the Works Progress Administration encourages workers to labor for America and for prosperity. It shows a farmer and a mechanical laborer shaking hands, symbolizing their common desire for steady work. Created by the Federal Arts Project between 1936 and 1941.

Dorothea Lange, Resettlement Administration photographer, in California, February 1936, just a month before she took her most famous photograph.

Francisco. During the Great Depression, her interests shifted to the unfolding human tragedy. Lange began by taking her camera to the streets. There she photographed breadlines, soup kitchens, and protests by the unemployed. While documenting the lives of Dust Bowl refugees for the Farm Security Administration, she took what is perhaps the most famous image of Depression-era America. Titled "Migrant Mother," it is also a marvelous example of how photographs do not always tell the whole story of what they are supposed to portray. If only for that reason, "Migrant Mother" bears closer study.

In March 1936, Lange was driving home to San Francisco after completing a job. Along the way, she passed a crude sign announcing PEA-PICKERS CAMP. She kept going. Yet she could not forget the sign, or the stories that might lay behind it. Twenty minutes later, she made a U-turn on the empty highway. At the town of Nipomo, she turned onto a muddy road and found a camp with some 2,500 migrant workers. A cold snap had killed the pea crop, and they would have to search for work elsewhere.

Leaving her car, Lange saw a mother seated in a canvas lean-to with a baby in her arms and two other children huddled around her. The woman seemed stunned and despairing over her family's plight. Lange told what happened next:

> **I saw and approached the hungry and desperate mother, as if drawn by a magnet. I do not remember how I explained my presence or my camera to her, but I do remember she asked me no questions. . . . I did not ask her name or history. She told me her age, that she was thirty-two. She said that they had been living**

Florence Thompson and three of her children in a California camp. This 1936 photograph is known as "Migrant Mother." Within days of its release copies appeared in publications across the country.

Dorothea Lange (1895-1965) had a hard childhood. Born in Hoboken, New Jersey, she fell ill with polio at the age of seven and walked with a limp for the rest of her life. Dorothea took up photography as a teenager and was a natural. A critic recalled, "She could look at something: a line of laundry flapping in the wind, a pair of old, wrinkled, worn-out hands, a breadline, a crowd of people in a bus station, and find it beautiful. Her eye was a camera lens and her camera—as she put it—an 'appendage of the body.'"

Most famous for her marvelous photographs of Depression-era America, Lange continued to document American life into World War II, including a photographic record of the government's internment of Japanese-Americans. Eventually she went on to found a photography magazine called *Aperture*.

Of her work, Lange once said, "I am trying here to say something about the despised, the defeated, the alienated. About death and disaster, about the wounded, the crippled, the helpless, the rootless, the dislocated. About finality. About the last ditch."[7]

frozen vegetables from the surrounding fields, and birds that the children had killed. She had just sold the tires from her car to buy food. There she sat in that lean-to tent with her children huddled around her, and seemed to know that my pictures might help her, and so she helped me. There was a sort of equality about it.[4]

Forty years later, the two older children in Lange's photo remembered the incident differently. Their mother was Florence Owens Thompson, a full-blooded Native American who had left Oklahoma ten years earlier, and so was no Dust Bowl refugee, as the photo suggests. The family had not been living on frozen peas and dead birds. Nor had Mrs. Thompson sold her tires. Her husband had taken the car for repairs, and she had moved to the pea camp from another camp. Before leaving, she left word for her husband to come to the new location. She looked worried in the picture because she was not sure he got the message.

Lange, the children recalled, had promised not to publish the photo, but had done exactly that. It appeared on March 10, 1936, in the *San Francisco News*, above First Lady Eleanor Roosevelt's weekly "My Day" column. Thompson saw the picture and felt betrayed. For the rest of her life, she resented Lange's use of her image for publicity. Thompson was an active woman, who had helped organize farmworkers' unions. "She was a very strong woman," said daughter Katherine, seen in the photo by her mother's right shoulder. "She was a leader. I think that's one of the reasons she resented the photo—because it didn't show her in that light."[5] "What upsets us is that people are making money out of our mother's pain,"[6] said daughter Katherine. Yet Lange's photo and Lorentz's film, as well as works by other photographers, served a worthwhile purpose. Better than any printed speech, they taught Americans about the need to protect the land.

Hugh Bennett led a new federal agency, the Soil Conservation Service, into action. They set out to educate farmers and rehabilitate the drought-stricken plains. To combat soil erosion, conservation experts introduced contour plowing—or plowing furrows that followed the slope of the land instead of running in a straight line. Thus, when it rained, the curving furrows slowed drainage, allowing the ground to absorb more water. To hold down the soil, the Soil Conservation Service encouraged planting crops such as soybeans and sweet clover as substitutes for native grasses.

President Roosevelt went further. FDR used to describe himself as a "tree farmer," adding that "the forests are the lungs of our land, purifying our air and giving strength to our people." Indeed, the president, who loved trees almost as if they were his own children, put the power of his office behind the Shelterbelt Project. The government would pay farmers to allow the planting of 220 million trees on their land in a 100-mile-wide "shelterbelt" stretching from the Canadian border to the Texas Panhandle. Trees such as red cedar and green ash reduce the force of the wind and cool the surrounding area. This, in turn, limits the destructive effects of heat and drought.

By 1938, the new conservation methods championed by President Roosevelt and Hugh Bennett had reduced the amount of blowing soil by as much as half. But they had not ended the drought. Nature did that. In 1939, the rains returned.

First-graders, some of Japanese ancestry, pledging allegiance to the United States flag in San Francisco, California, April 1942. Children of Japanese ancestry were shortly to be removed from school and placed in internment centers for the duration of the war. Photograph by Dorothea Lange. Lange and other photographers were hired by the United States War Relocation Authority to document how humanely Japanese-Americans were treated as they were rounded up and relocated. However, Lange and many others did not see the forced internment as humane. In 1988 President Ronald Reagan apologized for Japanese-American internment and provided reparations of twenty thousand dollars to each victim.

An early use of contour farming, used to prevent rain from washing away fertile topsoil.

An aerial view of terracing to prevent erosion.

People still remember what it felt like. "When the rain came, it meant life itself," farmer Floyd Coen recalled. "It meant a future. It meant there would be something better ahead for you. And we as young people, and sometimes parents, you'd go out in that rain and just feel that rain hit your face. It was a—a very emotional time when you'd get rain because it meant so much to you. You didn't have false hope any more, you knew then that you were going to have some crops."[8]

As fields turned green and gold with ripening wheat, the Great Depression ended in an unexpected way. Japan had recently invaded China, and Germany had begun the Second World War in Europe. President Roosevelt saw war coming to America, as it finally did when Japanese forces attacked the naval base at Pearl Harbor on December 7, 1941. To prepare for the war he saw coming, in 1940 Roosevelt launched a massive armaments build-up. Each day, the government poured tens of millions of dollars into the defense industries. Factories that had lain idle for a decade, and countless new ones besides, sprang to life.

Not only did these factories need metal and rubber and chemicals for weapons, they needed workers. Practically overnight, unemployment ended and a labor shortage began. Wages skyrocketed. Dust Bowl refugees went from poverty to plenty. Most Okies left the fields for defense plants and shipyards. For them, too, the hard times were over. With money in their pockets, they could make the future better for their families.

OPPOSITE PAGE: A double assembly line of aircraft production, April 1943. The planes, Boeing B-24 heavy bombers, bear Air Force markings.

RISK OF HUMAN-INDUCED DESERTIFICATION

*Our impact on the planet continues to challenge nature.
An ever-growing world population requires more and more
farmland for food production, leading in turn to an increase in
soil erosion and the spread of desertification, setting the stage
for more dust bowls around the globe.*

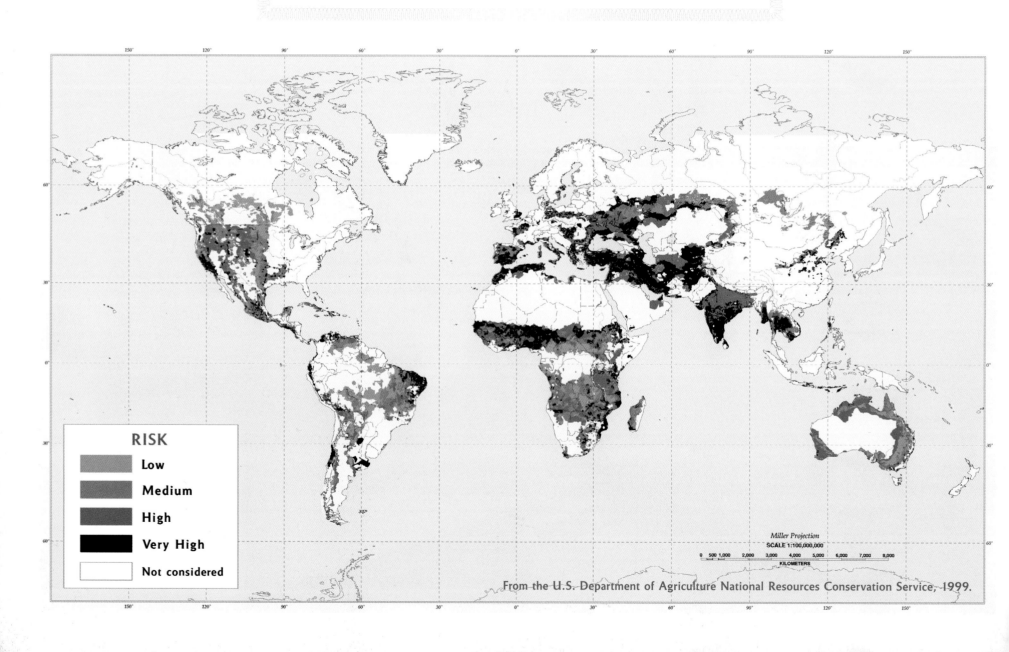

RISK

Low

Medium

High

Very High

Not considered

Miller Projection
SCALE 1:100,000,000

0   500 1,000   2,000   3,000   4,000   5,000   6,000   7,000   8,000
KILOMETERS

From the U.S. Department of Agriculture National Resources Conservation Service, 1999.

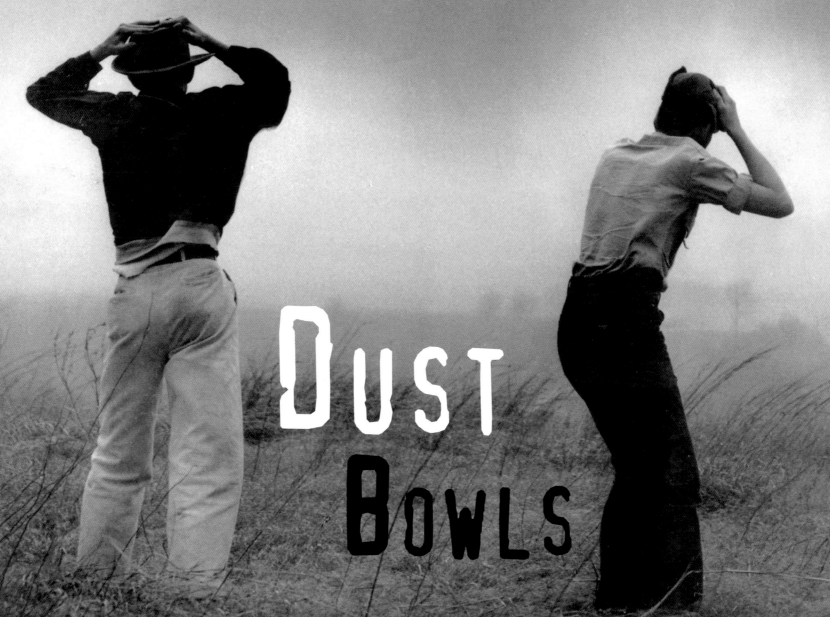

Future

Dust
Bowls

What is necessary for a new disaster is only for memories of the last one to fade, and no one knows how long that takes.

— JOHN KENNETH GALBRAITH, ECONOMIST AND
ADVISER TO PRESIDENT JOHN F. KENNEDY

ON A BRIGHT, COOL DAY in 1941, a group of Kansas wheat farmers gathered on the steps of their town courthouse. The drought was over and prosperity had returned to the Great Plains, so most were hopeful about the future. "People are thinking differently about taking care of the land," one said, smiling. The others nodded in agreement—all, that is, except one. "Don't fool yourself," he growled. "You can't convince me we've learned our lesson. It's just not in our blood to play a safe game." Time would prove this doubter right.[1]

During the Second World War, American food aid helped the embattled Allies, Great Britain and the Soviet Union, survive. After the Allied victory in 1945, food grown on the Great Plains enabled war-torn Europe to recover. As wheat prices rose in the United States, however, many farmers acted as if the Dust Bowl had never happened. As with the Great Plow-Up a generation earlier, they ignored soil conservation and did whatever they could to boost production. A new generation of tractors, faster and more powerful than ever, pulled 42-foot disk plows. By the fall of 1946, farmers had plowed

PREVIOUS PAGE: Two men hold on to their hats during a dust storm near Topeka, Kansas, in 1950.
RIGHT: A worker for the Civilian Conservation Corps planting a pine tree in Lolo National Forest, Montana, 1938. Most CCC workers were unemployed youths from Depression-ravaged cities.

Restoring the Land

In 1990, Native Americans formed the Intertribal Bison Cooperative (ITBC). Its aim is "to restore bison to Indian Nations in a manner that is compatible with their spiritual and cultural beliefs and practices." Today, ITBC members have over eight thousand buffalo in their herds. The tribes have also made a major effort to replant the native grasses the buffalo feed upon. The photograph above shows big bluestem, a grass native to the Great Plains region which can grow up to ten feet tall. Big bluestem was an important grass for bison and is also good forage for cattle and horses. The bluestem species is prized by ecologists working to restore the prairie because its strong, deep roots help to form tough sod and protect the land from erosion.

under another four million acres of grassland. Some grass was the original sod, the rest, grass that had grown on lands abandoned in the thirties. Eager for more cropland and dollars, farmers also tore out millions of shelterbelt trees. Profits soared.[2]

The good times could not last forever; they never do, particularly on the Great Plains. In 1952, farmers saw a replay of the dirty thirties. They called it the "filthy fifties." Drought and record heat waves returned, and with them dust storms. In 1945, just one major dust storm rolled across the plains; in 1952, there were ten. For the next five years, until the rains returned, crops wilted, cattle starved, highways became impassable, and people died of dust pneumonia. Had the drought continued longer, another full-scale Dust Bowl might have occurred. Drought returned in 1974, and again dust storms raged. Luckily, this drought lasted "only" three years.

In a drought that lasted from 1998 to 2002, rainfall was 30 percent less than what fell during the thirties. Yet the dust storms did not compare to those of the past. One reason is that many farmers have accepted government payments to take land out of production, allowing it to return to grass. The lesson is clear: serious droughts are inevitable. We should expect them and plan for them. If not, we will see more Dust Bowls.[3]

History is more than a record of politics, wars, and economic changes. It is also an encyclopedia of human folly and lessons for the future. Seen in this light, the Dust Bowl has serious implications not only for Americans, but for all people. As world population grows in

OPPOSITE PAGE: Grass seeds are placed in dishes for germination testing at the NRCS National Plant Materials Center, where plants and technologies are developed to restore wildlife habitat, protect soil against erosion, and otherwise help to conserve natural resources.

President Roosevelt's shelterbelt of trees was not a complete success and was never finished. After the drought ended and rains returned to the Great Plains, the price of wheat went up. Farmers then cut down shelterbelt trees to get more land for planting. This poster, created by the Illinois WPA (Works Projects Administration) in the late 1930s, encourages the planting of trees to prevent wind erosion, ease drought, and promote healthier plains farms.

OPPOSITE PAGE: This chart shows a dramatic increase in severe dust storms in China. From Dust in the Wind: Desertification and Dust Storms in China by T. Goulbourne, K. Twanmoh, and W. Zhou, Columbia University, 2005.

the twenty-first century, humanity will place greater demands on nature. However, nature operates according to its own laws, which have nothing to do with our needs and desires. Whether we like it or not, we are bound by nature's laws. If the Dust Bowl experience teaches anything, it is that the natural world is not merely a "resource" humans can exploit for profit, without thought for the consequences.

In 2001, a news report from China had an ominous tone. "The rising sands," it said, "are part of a new desert forming here on the eastern edge of the Quinghai-Tibet Plateau, a legendary stretch once known for grass reaching as high as a horse's belly and home for centuries to ethnic Tibetan herders."

China offers a striking example of desertification; that is, turning fertile land into desert. In the northwest and near Tibet on the Indian border, China has grasslands similar to the Great Plains of North America. For thousands of years, natives of these grasslands herded cattle, goats, and sheep on horseback. Nomads, they moved from place to place in search of pasture for their herds. Like the Plains Indian buffalo hunters, they never stayed in one place long enough to harm the environment. For China's grasslands, too, have years-long dry spells followed by years of plentiful rain. Moreover, like the Great Plains, they have windstorms, which pick up loose soil. These dust storms are normal, and people have learned to expect them and live with them.

With over 1.3 billion people, China's population is nearly five times that of the United States. As its population grows, its cities grow, too. This growth, in turn, demands ever more land for housing, industry, and transportation. In 1994, the Chinese government made a critical

A New Dust Bowl?

The grasslands that cover 40 percent of China are the largest area in the world currently threatened by desertification. Scientists estimate that 90 percent of China's grasslands have suffered some extent of erosion, largely due to grazing and farming practices, as well as the growth of cities into once rural areas. Dust and sand storms are now serious problems in the region, bringing economic hardship and health trouble to many Chinese. To combat the ecological disaster, China planted trees. Shelterbelt programs that were started in the 1950s had more than doubled China's forest coverage by 2002. More recent efforts to combat desertification include windbreaks, soil conservation, control of water erosion and community development projects.[4] But the storms continue to grow.

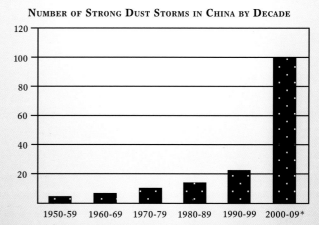

NUMBER OF STRONG DUST STORMS IN CHINA BY DECADE

*This is a preliminary estimate for the decade based on more than 20 storms in 2000 and 2001.

The Great Plains Today

Drought returned to the Great Plains in the 1970s and from 2000 to 2003. But the devastating erosion and storms of the Dust Bowl did not return in force. Studies show that the soil conservation methods first championed by Hugh Bennett and Franklin D. Roosevelt are still helping to keep the soil in place. Today, conservationists continue to fight erosion. According to the Department of Agriculture, soil erosion on United States cropland was reduced by 43 percent from 1982 to 2003. But farming the land still takes a toll. In 2003 scientists estimated that 28 percent of all U.S. cropland continued to erode "above soil loss tolerance rates"—too quickly.

An American flag created on the landscape of a farm during the Dust Bowl days. This photograph and many others concerning historic and present-day ecology in America can be viewed at the NRCS (National Resources Conservation Service) online photo gallery.

decision in order to feed the country's growing population. It ordered that, for every acre of farmland taken for city expansion, another acre of farmland must replace it elsewhere. That new land would have to come from China's grasslands. Thus, plows tore into lands that are regularly exposed to heat, drought, and wind. While the plows did their work, expanding livestock herds stripped yet more of the land of vegetation. China now has more than 127 million cattle, versus 98 million in the United States. Its sheep and goats number 279 million, versus nine million in the United States. When we think of cowboys, the legendary American cowboy immediately comes to mind. Today, however, the typical cowboy is Chinese.

The result of China's expanding farming and grazing operations has been an ecological disaster. Official Chinese government reports estimate that 900 square miles of grassland are turning into desert every year. The Dust Bowl of the dirty thirties has returned, only on the other side of the planet. Dust storms whipped up in China's ruined grasslands affect some 100 million people. Often the storms blanket Beijing in gritty, brownish mists. The dust hides the sun, slows traffic to a crawl, and closes airports. It crunches between people's teeth, makes them sneeze, and brings tears to their eyes. City residents tape their doors and windows shut, and sleep on damp sheets.

In March 2002, an immense dust cloud from China reached South Korea. Officials in Seoul, the capital, ordered anyone with breathing problems to stay indoors, or to wear a face mask outdoors. The cloud continued to drift eastward, over the Sea of Japan, over Japan, and over the Pacific Ocean. In April, scientists at the National Oceanic and Atmospheric Administration laboratory in Boulder, Colorado,

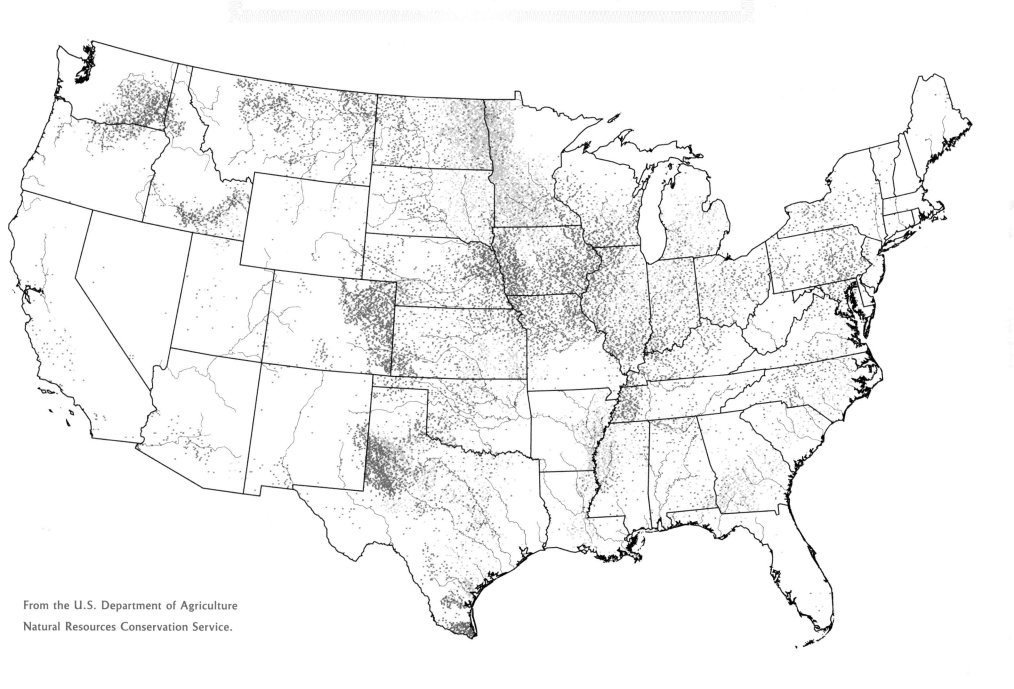

EXCESSIVE EROSION ON CROPLAND, 1997

Each gray dot represents 5,000 acres of land with excess erosion above the "tolerable" soil erosion rate. 108 million acres show excessive erosion, with a total of 1.3 billion tons of soil erosion.

From the U.S. Department of Agriculture

Natural Resources Conservation Service.

The cedars of Lebanon, near Tripoli. The Lebanon cedar was an important tree to many civilizations, including the ancient Egyptians, Jews, Babylonians, Greeks, and Romans, and is an emblem on the modern Lebanese flag. Centuries of deforestation once threatened the cedar forests, which are now expanding due to massive replanting and efforts to protect seedlings.

reported the cloud "blanketing areas from Canada to Arizona with a layer of dust." Along the foothills of the Rockies, the mountains were hidden by the dusty haze from China.[5]

What to do? Chinese scientists advise their government as Hugh Bennett once advised President Roosevelt:

> **The options are clear: reduce livestock populations to a sustainable level or face heavy livestock losses as grassland turns to desert. Return highly erodible cropland to grassland or lose all of the land's productive capacity as it turns to desert. Construct windbreaks with a combination of trees and, where feasible, wind turbines, to slow the wind or face even more losses and dust storms.[6]**

Despite China's efforts to slow desertification and destruction of grassland, dust storms there are on the rise.

Africa's Sahel region is another danger spot for a new dust bowl. The Sahel is a wide band of land running eastward from the Atlantic Ocean to the Indian Ocean. An area larger than the continental United States, it includes the countries of Senegal, Mauritania, Mali, Burkina Faso, Niger, Nigeria, Chad, Sudan, and Eritrea.

Sahel is the Arabic word for "edge" or "fringe." It is a good name, for the region lies between the Sahara (the Arabic word for "desert") to the north and the more tropical areas to the south. The Sahel receives only six to ten inches of rainfall a year, mostly from clouds drifting inland from the Indian Ocean. Thus, it can only support short grasses and acacias, types of spiny shrubs and trees able to survive on little water.

For centuries, the peoples of the northern Sahel lived in harmony with nature. Experience had taught them never to plant the same field more than three years in a row, because crops take nutrients such as nitrogen from the soil, reducing its fertility. Instead, they allowed fields to rest, or lay fallow, for a year or so. During that time, wild plants took over, died, decayed, and replaced the nutrients. To further increase fertility, farmers grazed their cattle and goats on the wild plants. The manure of these animals, like the buffaloes' on the Great Plains, further enriched the soil. Between planting and harvesting, herdsmen took the villagers' livestock to graze in open country. Herdsmen allowed the animals to eat grass, but were careful to keep them away from the acacias, because their roots anchored the soil. Bands of nomads grazed their animals in the same way.

Just as the "filthy fifties" were opening on the Great Plains of North America, the Sahel was enjoying a long stretch of abundant rainfall. Governments saw a chance to raise much-needed money by "developing" the region and selling its farm products to Europe. So they urged many farmers to move northward, closer to the Sahara. Outsiders brought more livestock and plowed the grass under to plant cash crops: peanuts, cotton, melons, and sorghum, a cereal grass resembling corn. Meanwhile, governments raised taxes on the natives of the fringe-lands, forcing them to earn more money. To increase production, farmers broke with tradition. They no longer left fields fallow, but planted the same crops year after year. Overstocking the fragile land compacted the soil and reduced its ability to hold water, as cattle had done on the American Great Plains. Villagers cut the acacias for firewood. Desertification followed.

Two men plowing with oxen during a five-year drought in the Sahelian Zone of West Africa. Scientists estimate that 90 percent of West Africa's rain forests have disappeared since 1900. Beginning in 1968, a five-year drought and accompanying desertification in the Sahel resulted in widespread famine and the collapse of agriculture in five African countries.

Drought comes to the Sahel when the moisture-bearing winds blowing inland from the Indian Ocean weaken or change direction. In the years 1968 to 1973, the region suffered its worst drought on record. It was so dry that the Sahara Desert "migrated" southward several feet a year, simply burying farms; in Mali, it buried entire villages. Lands already damaged by human abuse became true dust bowls, complete with sandstorms and swarms of locusts that hid the sun and ate anything they could bite into. The resulting famine claimed the lives of as many as a million people and five million farm animals. As during the last days of the buffalo, the lands of the northern Sahel glistened with sun-bleached bones. Although the rains have since returned, everyone knows drought will surely return, too. People wonder if (or when) land abuse and drought will turn the entire Sahel into part of the Sahara.[7]

Desertification also threatens large areas of the Amazon rain forest in South America. A rain forest is a large, very dense forest in a region where rain is heavy throughout the year. Flowing eastward from the Andes Mountains, the Amazon River contains one-fifth of the combined water in all our planet's rivers. Covering 2.3 million square miles on both sides of the Amazon, the rain forest stretches over parts of Brazil, Venezuela, Colombia, Ecuador, and Peru. This forest produces 20 percent of the world's oxygen, thus the nickname "the lungs of the earth." The air that people and animals breathe out of their lungs contains carbon dioxide, a colorless, odorless gas. Plants absorb carbon dioxide through their leaves, use it to grow themselves, and then send oxygen back into the air for us to breathe in.

OPPOSITE PAGE: Indian rubber gatherers on the upper Amazon, Brazil, between 1890 and 1923.

The Great Green Wall

Echoing President Roosevelt's Great Plains shelterbelt, which once stretched over 18,000 miles of prairie, countries around the world are turning to trees to fight desertification and dust storms. In 2008, nations of the African Sahel began work on a "Green Wall," a ten-mile-wide line of trees that many hope will help to fight the spread of the Sahara Desert. The massive Green Wall is planned to reach from western to eastern Africa. In Asia, the "Green Wall of China" or the "Great Green Wall" is also underway in an effort to hold back the encroaching Gobi Desert. The Great Green Wall is projected to be finished by 2072 and stretch more than 2,800 miles. Experts warn that planting trees is just one step in many that must be taken to combat desertification and erosion. Below, smaller windbreaks formed by trees help to protect farmland in North Dakota.

The Black-footed Ferret

Thanks to restoration efforts that began in the 1930s, three national grasslands now exist in what was once America's Dust Bowl. Some animals, like the buffalo and the bald eagle, have begun to make a comeback from the brink of extinction. But other species of prairie wildlife are still struggling. The black-footed ferret is a small, wiry animal that lived in prairie grassland and preyed on prairie dogs. Due largely to loss of habitat, this ferret is now one of the most endangered mammals in North America. Once feared extinct, the last-known group of black-footed ferrets in the wild was taken into captivity in the 1980s. Since then, scientists have been releasing ferrets bred in captivity into the wild in hopes of restoring the population.

About half the world's plant and animal species live in the Amazon rain forest. This includes 56,000 species of plants, 1,700 of birds, 1,345 of amphibians and reptiles (frogs, lizards, snakes), and 578 species of mammals. Scientists have derived many drugs to cure illnesses from the rain forest's plants and animals. Curare, for example, is a plant poison that forest Indians put on the points of their hunting arrows. Surgeons use curare-based medicines to relax patients' muscles during operations. Indians also rub their arrowheads along the backs of poisonous tree frogs. While the tree frog's poison kills by paralyzing nerves, used judiciously it can also block pain better and more safely than habit-forming drugs like morphine.[8] Further discoveries await as scientists find new species of plants and animals in the scarcely explored region, but these advances in science are threatened by the destruction of the rain forest.

The Amazon rain forest covers 60 percent of the surface of Brazil, South America's largest country. And it is dying. Farmers, ranchers, and loggers often see the forest as a treasure house they can freely plunder. Although the Brazilian government allows logging only in certain parts of the rain forest, illegal cutting—especially of mahogany and other valuable trees—is widespread. Since 74 percent of Europe's imported beef comes from Brazil, its ranchers treat the rain forest as "free range," land they just have to clear for pasture. According to the Brazilian version of the U.S. Homestead Act, a person can own rain forest land by "using" it for five years. Beginning in the late 1970s, thousands of poor families and big farming companies have moved into the rain forest every year, clearing the vegetation with fires visible from space. In 2004, satellite pictures showed 600 fires burning in the rain forest each day. Between 1978 and 2005, fires destroyed 211,180 square miles of Amazon rain forest. Put differently, forest equal to six football fields goes up in smoke every minute. At this rate, the rain forest could be wiped out in forty years.[9]

The destruction of the Amazon rain forest has serious consequences that we are just beginning to understand. Brazilian farmers plant cleared land with cash crops: bananas, corn, rice, soybeans. After a few years, the soil loses nutrients, production falls, and farmers clear more forest, leaving the ruined fields as wasteland.

This wasteland doesn't only breed dust storms that affect the region. Massive deforestation in the Amazon may influence the climate of the United States. It may even set the stage for another American dust bowl. Here's why: forested lands hold rainwater. Gradually, the water in the forest will evaporate and form a raincloud. Wind or a jet stream can carry the moisture laden clouds to other parts of the globe. However, removing the tree cover allows rainwater to run off quickly into streams, lessening the amount of moisture released into the atmosphere. Thus, destroying the Amazon rain forest may reduce summer rainfall along the Gulf of Mexico and on the American Great Plains. "What this suggests," says Duke University scientist Roni Avissar, "is that if you mess up the planet at one point, the impact could have far-reaching effects."[10]

In other words, there are no true "islands." While separated by distance, every thing and every person is bound together in ways we do not fully understand. So, what happens in one place may well affect what happens far away. Storms in China bring dust to the

The only known photograph of Chief Seattle, taken in 1864 by E. M. Sammis.

Praying to the spirits at Crater Lake, Oregon, c. 1923.

Rocky Mountains. Deforestation in South America leads to drought on America's Great Plains. Rapid consumption of goods and energy in America has consequences that reach around the globe.

The worst tragedies in history have owed more to human folly than to nature. But what has been, need not be forever. People make their history—it does not make them. Thus, we can and must find ways to satisfy our needs without so damaging the environment as to make it incapable of supporting life. Humans, who can split the atom and go into space, can also use their reason to protect the natural world.

Chief Seattle, a leader of the Suquamish tribe, understood our place in nature. In 1855, President Franklin Pierce offered to buy Suquamish lands in what is now the state of Washington. Before accepting the president's terms, Seattle is said to have reminded the American envoys of some basic truths. "Will you teach your children what we have taught our children? That the earth is our mother?" the chief asked. Then Seattle answered his own questions. "What befalls the earth befalls the sons of the earth. . . . The earth does not belong to man, man belongs to the earth. . . . All things are connected like the blood which unites us all. Man did not weave the web of life, he is merely a strand in it. Whatever he does to the web, he does to himself."[11]

We should remember the wise chief's words when we think about the Dust Bowl that was and the dust bowls that yet may be.

Words to Know

AGRONOMIST * an expert in soil management and methods of increasing crop production.

AQUIFER * an underground layer of rock, gravel, or sand in which water collects. The Ogallala Aquifer beneath the Great Plains is the largest in the United States.

DESERTIFICATION * the process of desert formation, during which drought causes the top layers of soil to dry out and the wind blows the dust away.

DROUGHT * a period of time when little or no rain falls.

DUST * soil, sand, or other matter in fine, dry particles.

DUST BOWL * the name given to those areas of the Great Plains most devastated by the dust storms of the 1930s.

DUST STORM * a cloud of dust raised and blown by wind.

ECOSYSTEM * a community of living things—plants and animals, including humans—and their physical surroundings.

EROSION * the wearing away of land, often by the forces of wind and water, causing soil to move from one place to another.

GREAT DEPRESSION (1929-1940) * when the U.S. economy, and most of the world economy, came to a near-standstill, putting millions of people out of work.

HEAT WAVE * an extended period of extreme heat, often accompanied by high humidity.

JET STREAM * a strong wind current usually blowing between seven and nine miles above the earth's surface, moving in a west-to-east direction at speeds of 80 to 190 miles an hour. Jet streams are thousands of miles long and hundreds of miles wide.

MORTGAGE * a loan, usually from a bank, to buy property.

NEW DEAL * the programs introduced by President Franklin D. Roosevelt to limit the effects of the Great Depression, help those who suffered most from its ravages, and enable the economy to recover.

OKIES * a term, usually mocking, used to describe Oklahoma farmers "blown out" of their land by dust storms and forced to seek work in California.

SHARECROPPER * a farmer who gives a landowner part of the harvest in exchange for being allowed to farm the owner's land.

TENANT FARMER * a farmer who rents land from the landowner for money.

WHITEOUT * when fast-falling snow makes it impossible to see or take your bearing from landmarks.

123

NOTES

PROLOGUE: DARKNESS AT NOON
1. Donald Worster, *Dust Bowl: The Southern Plains in the 1930s* (New York: Oxford University Press, 1979), 28.
2. *Ibid.*, 46.

I · THE GREAT PLAINS WORLD
1. T. H. Watkins, *The Hungry Years: A Narrative History of the Great Depression in America* (New York: Henry Holt Co., 1999), 424.
2. Jon E. Lewis, *The West: The Making of the American West* (New York: Carroll & Graf, 2001), 463.
3. Joanna L. Stratton, *Pioneer Women: Voices from the Kansas Frontier* (New York: Touchstone, 1981), 104.

II · CONQUERING THE GREAT PLAINS
1. "The Lewis and Clark Journey of Discovery," www.nps.gov/jeff/LewisClark2/The Journey/Geography.htm.
2. Ray Allen Billington and Martin Ridge, *Westward Expansion: A History of the American Frontier* (New York: Macmillan Publishing Co., 1982), 395.
3. Wayne Gard, *The Great Buffalo Hunt* (New York: Knopf, 1960), 215.
4. Theodore Roosevelt, *Hunting Expeditions in the West* (New York: G. P. Putnam's Sons, 1927), 186–187.
5. *Ibid.*, 223–224; Norman B. Wiltsey, *Brave Warriors* (Caldwell, ID: The Caxton Printers, 1963), 262.
6. Walter Prescott Webb, *The Great Plains* (Boston: Ginn & Company, 1931), 11.
7. Hermann Hagedorn, *Roosevelt in the Bad Lands* (Boston: Houghton Mifflin Company, 1921), 433.
8. Edmund Morris, *The Rise of Theodore Roosevelt* (New York: Coward, McCann & Geoghegan, 1979), 372.
9. "Last Buffalo Killed in North Dakota," American Memory, http://lcweb2.loc.gov.

III · THE COMING OF THE FARMERS
1. Billington & Ridge, *Westward Expansion*, 646–647.
2. R. Douglas Hurt, *The Dust Bowl: An Agricultural and Social History* (Chicago: Nelson-Hall, 1984), 7–8.
3. "Planet Gobbling Dust Storms," http://science.nasa.gov.
4. "The American Experience: Surviving the Dust Bowl," www.pbs.org/wgbh/pages/amex/dustbowl.
5. "Let's Go for a Spin," American Memory, http://lcweb2.loc.gov.

IV · IN HARD TIMES
1. Donald Worster, *Under Western Skies: Nature and History in the American West* (New York: Oxford University Press), 1992, 99.3
2. Woody Guthrie, "Pretty Boy Floyd," www.woodyguthrie.org.

V · DUST BOWL DAYS
1. "Hugh Hammond Bennett" in "The American Experience: Surviving the Dust Bowl," www.pbs.org/wgbh/pages/amex/dustbowl.
2. "The Hopi Snake Dance," *A Book Lover's Holidays in the Open* (New York: Scribners, 1916).
3. Edward Robb Ellis, *A Nation in Torment: The Great American Depression, 1929–1939* (New York: Kodansha International, 1995), 457–458.
4. *Ibid.*, 454.
5. T. H. Watkins, *The Great Depression: America in the 1930s* (Boston: Little, Brown and Company, 1993), 191.
6. Timothy Egan, *The Worst Hard Time: The Untold Story of Those Who Survived the Great American Dust Bowl* (Boston: Houghton Mifflin, 2005), 153, 172.
7. Frank L. Stallings, Jr. *Black Sunday: The Great Dust Storm of April 14, 1935* (Austin, TX: Eakin Press, 2001), 114, 135.
8. *Ibid.*, 66–67.
9. *Ibid.*, 136.
10. "The Drought," www.pbs.org/wgbh/amex/dustbowl.
11. Worster, *Dust Bowl*, 17.
12. *Ibid.*, 15, 23.
13. T. Egan, *The Worst Hard Time*, 174.
14. Ann Marie Low, *Dust Bowl Diary* (Lincoln: University of Nebraska Press, 1984), 96–98.
15. William Manchester, *The Glory and the Dream: A Narrative History of America, 1932–1972* (Boston: Little, Brown and Company, 1974), 119.
16. Glenn D. McMurry, "The Autobiography of an Unimportant Man," www.gregssandbox.com/mcmurry.
17. Ellis, *A Nation in Torment*, 456.
18. Woody Guthrie, "Dust Pneumonia," http://sniff.numachi.com.
19. T. Egan. *The Worst Hard Time*.
20. Caroline Henderson, *Letters from the Dust Bowl* (Norman: University of Oklahoma, 2001), 164.
21. Worster, *Dust Bowl*, 23.
22. R. Douglas Hurt, *Dust Bowl*, 58; Worster, *Dust Bowl*, 23; Watkins, *Hungry Years*, 430.

VI · REFUGEES IN THEIR OWN LAND
1. Watkins, *The Great Depression*, 70.
2. Clifford R. Hope, Sr., "Kansas in the 1930s," *Kansas Historical Quarterly*, Spring 1970, 1–12, http://kshs.org.
3. Woody Guthrie, "The Great Dust Storm," www.woodyguthrie.org.
4. John Steinbeck, *The Grapes of Wrath* (New York: Viking, 1939), 121.
5. *Ibid.*
6. Watkins, *The Hungry Years*, 436.
7. Jerry Stanley, *Children of the Dust Bowl: The True Story of the School at Weedpatch Camp* (New York: Crown Publishers, 1992), 22.
8. T. Egan. *The Worst Hard Time*, 238, 254.

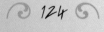

9. Ellis, *A Nation in Torment*, 460.
10. Steinbeck, *The Grapes of Wrath*.
11. Milton Meltzer, *Brother Can You Spare a Dime? The Great Depression, 1929–1933* (New York: Alfred A. Knopf, 1969), 140.
12. Worster, *Dust Bowl*, 53.
13. Watkins, *The Hungry Years*, 202.

VII • THE NEW DEAL

1. John Steinbeck, *Harvest Gypsies*, quoted in Michael L. Cooper, *Dust to Eat: Drought and Depression in the 1930s* (New York: Clarion, 2004), 52.
2. David M. Kennedy, *Freedom from Fear: The American People in Depression and War, 1929–1945* (New York: Oxford University Press, 1999), 205.
3. Maurice G. Cook, "Hugh Hammond Bennett: The Father of Soil Conservation," www.soil.ncsu.edu.
4. "Exploring Contexts: 'Migrant Mother,'" http://memory.loc.gov.
5. The children were Thompson's daughters Katherine McIntosh and Norma Rydlewski. "Exploring Contexts: 'Migrant Mother.'" See also Geoffrey Dunn, "Photographic License," *New Times* (San Luis Obispo, CA.), www.newtimes-slo.com.
6. "Dorothea Lange," www.spartacus.schoolnet.co.uk.
7. "Guide to Lange (Dorothea) Collection," *Online Archive of California*, www.oac.cdlib.org.
8. "The American Experience: Surviving the Dust Bowl."

VIII • FUTURE DUST BOWLS

1. "The American Experience: Surviving the Dust Bowl."
2. Worster, *Dust Bowl*, 226.
3. "Dry High Plains Are Blowing Away, Again," *New York Times*, May 3, 2002; "The New Dust Bowl," *Time*, September 16, 2002.
4. Natalie Meyer. "Desertification and Restoration of Grasslands in Inner Mongolia, China," 2005. http://forestry.msu.edu/China/New%20Folder/Natalie-Grasslands.pdf.
5. "Dust Bowl Threatening China's Future," International Erosion Control Association White Paper, www.ieca.org.
6. Lester R. Brown, "Another One Bites the Dust: China's Dust Bowl Is Growing at an Alarming Rate," *Grist Magazine*, May 29, 2002, www.grist.org.
7. Laurie J. Schmidt, "From the Dust Bowl to the Sahel," NASA Earth Science Enterprise, http://earthobservatory.nasa.gov/Study/DustBowl; "Sahel Africa," http://maps.unomaha.edu.
8. "Tropical Rainforests," http://rainforests.mongabay.com.
9. Charles J. Hanley, "Amazon Deforestation Adds to Warming Trend," Associated Press, February 16, 2005, www.msnbc.msn.com/id/6870856/.
10. Keith Lawrence, "Amazon Deforestation Could Affect U.S. Climate," Duke University News & Communications, October 24, 2002, www.dukenews.duke.edu/2002/10/avissar1024_print.htm.
11. Al Gore, *Earth in the Balance: Ecology and the Human Spirit* (New York: Penguin Books, 1993), 259.

BOOKS FOR KIDS

NONFICTION ❧

Cooper, Michael L. *Dust to Eat: Drought and Depression in the 1930s*. New York: Clarion, 2004.

Freedman, Russell. *Children of the Great Depression*. New York: Clarion, 2005.

Gore, Al. *An Inconvenient Truth: The Crises of Global Warming*. New York: Viking Children's Books, 2007.

Stanley, Jerry. *Children of the Dust Bowl: The True Story of the School at Weedpatch Camp*. New York: Crown, 1993.

FOR TEENS:

Egan, Timothy. *The Worst Hard Time: The Untold True Story of Those Who Survived the Great American Dust Bowl*. Boston: Houghton Mifflin, 2005.

LITERATURE ❧

Cather, Willa. *My Antonia*. Boston: Houghton Mifflin, 1995.

Hesse, Karen. *Out of the Dust*. New York: Scholastic, 1997.

McDunn, Rosemary. *The Green Coat: Tales from the Dust Bowl Years*. Michigan: Bezalel, 2007.

FOR TEENS:

Steinbeck, John. *The Grapes of Wrath*. New York: Viking, 1939.

125

BIBLIOGRAPHY

BOOKS AND ARTICLES

Billington, Ray Allen, and Ridge, Martin. *Westward Expansion: A History of the American Frontier.* New York: Macmillan Publishing Co., 1982.

Cook, Maurice G. "Hugh Hammond Bennett: The Father of Soil Conservation," *http://www.soil.ncsu.edu.*

Cooper, Michael L. *Dust to Eat: Drought and Depression in the 1930s.* New York: Clarion Books, 2004.

Egan, Timothy. *The Worst Hard Time: The Untold Story of Those Who Survived the Great American Dust Bowl.* Boston: Houghton Mifflin, 2005.

Ellis, Edward Robb. *A Nation in Torment: The Great American Depression, 1929–1939.* New York: Kodansha International, 1995.

Gore, Al. *Earth in the Balance: Ecology and the Human Spirit.* New York: Penguin Books, 1993.

Hagedorn, Hermann. *Roosevelt in the Bad Lands.* Boston: Houghton Mifflin Company, 1921.

Henderson, Caroline. *Letters from the Dust Bowl.* Norman: University of Oklahoma, 2001.

Hine, Robert V. and Faracher, John Mack. *The American West: A New Interpretive History.* New Haven: Yale University Press, 2000.

Hope, Clifford R., Sr., "Kansas in the 1930s," *Kansas Historical Quarterly*, Spring 1970, 1–12.

Howarth, William. "The Okies: Beyond the Dust Bowl," *National Geographic*, September, 1984, 322–349.

Hurt, R. Douglas. *The Dust Bowl: An Agricultural and Social History.* Chicago: Nelson-Hall, 1984.

Lewis, Jon E. *The West: The Making of the American West.* New York: Carroll & Graf, 2001.

Lockwood, Jeffrey, "The Death of the Super Hopper," *High Country News*: www.hcn.org/issues/243/13695

Low, Ann Marie. *Dust Bowl Diary.* Lincoln: University of Nebraska Press, 1984.

Manchester, William. *The Glory and the Dream: A Narrative History of America, 1932–1972.* Boston: Little, Brown and Company, 1974.

Parfit, Michael. "The Dust Bowl," *Smithsonian*, June 1989, 44–57.

Stallings, Frank L., Jr. *Black Sunday: The Great Dust Storm of April 14, 1935.* Austin, TX: Eakin Press, 2001.

Stanley, Jerry. *Children of the Dust Bowl: The True Story of the School at Weedpatch Camp.* New York: Crown Publishers, 1992.

Steinbeck, John. *The Grapes of Wrath.* New York: Viking, 1963.

———*The Harvest Gypsies: On the Road to the Grapes of Wrath.* Berkeley, CA.: Heyday Books, 1988.

Stratton, Joanna L. *Pioneer Women: Voices from the Kansas Frontier.* New York: Touchstone, 1981.

Watkins, T. H. *The Great Depression: America in the 1930s.* Boston: Little, Brown and Company, 1993.

———*The Hungry Years: A Narrative History of the Great Depression in America.* New York: Henry Holt and Company, 1999.

Webb, Walter Prescott. *The Great Plains.* Boston: Ginn & Company, 1931.

Worster, Donald. *Dust Bowl: The Southern Plains in the 1930s.* New York: Oxford University Press, 1979.

———*Under Western Skies: Nature and History in the American West.* New York: Oxford University Press, 1992.

PHOTOGRAPHY

Ganzel, Bill. *Dust Bowl Descent.* Lincoln: University of Nebraska Press, 1984.

Lange, Dorothea, and Taylor, Paul S. *An American Exodus: A Record of Human Erosion.* New York: Reynal and Hitchcock, 1940. Revised Edition: Yale University Press, 1969. A classic.

Rothstein, Arthur. *The Depression Years.* New York: Dover, 1978.

The online catalogs of the Library of Congress, the Franklin D. Roosevelt Library, and the National Resources Conservation Service: www.loc.gov; www.fdrlibrary.marist.edu; www.nrcs.usda.gov.

FILM

The Grapes of Wrath. A dramatization of John Steinbeck's novel about the plight of Oklahoma Dust Bowl refugees.

Surviving the Dust Bowl, written and produced by Chana Gazit, co-produced and edited by David Steward. A film for "The American Experience" series, a production of WGBH Boston, MA. 1998. www.pbs.org/wgbh/amex/dustbowl/filmmore
This site has the transcript of the film, plus additional material. Very valuable source.

The Plow That Broke the Plains, produced by Pare Lorentz, 1936. A U.S. Government Film.

MUSIC

"Woody Guthrie—Dust Bowl Ballads," Rounder Records (Rounder CD 1 040).

WEBSITE

"The American Experience: Surviving the Dust Bowl" www.pbs.org/wgbh/pages/amex/dustbowl/
This site has the program's film.

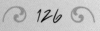

INDEX

Page numbers in *italics* refer to illustrations.

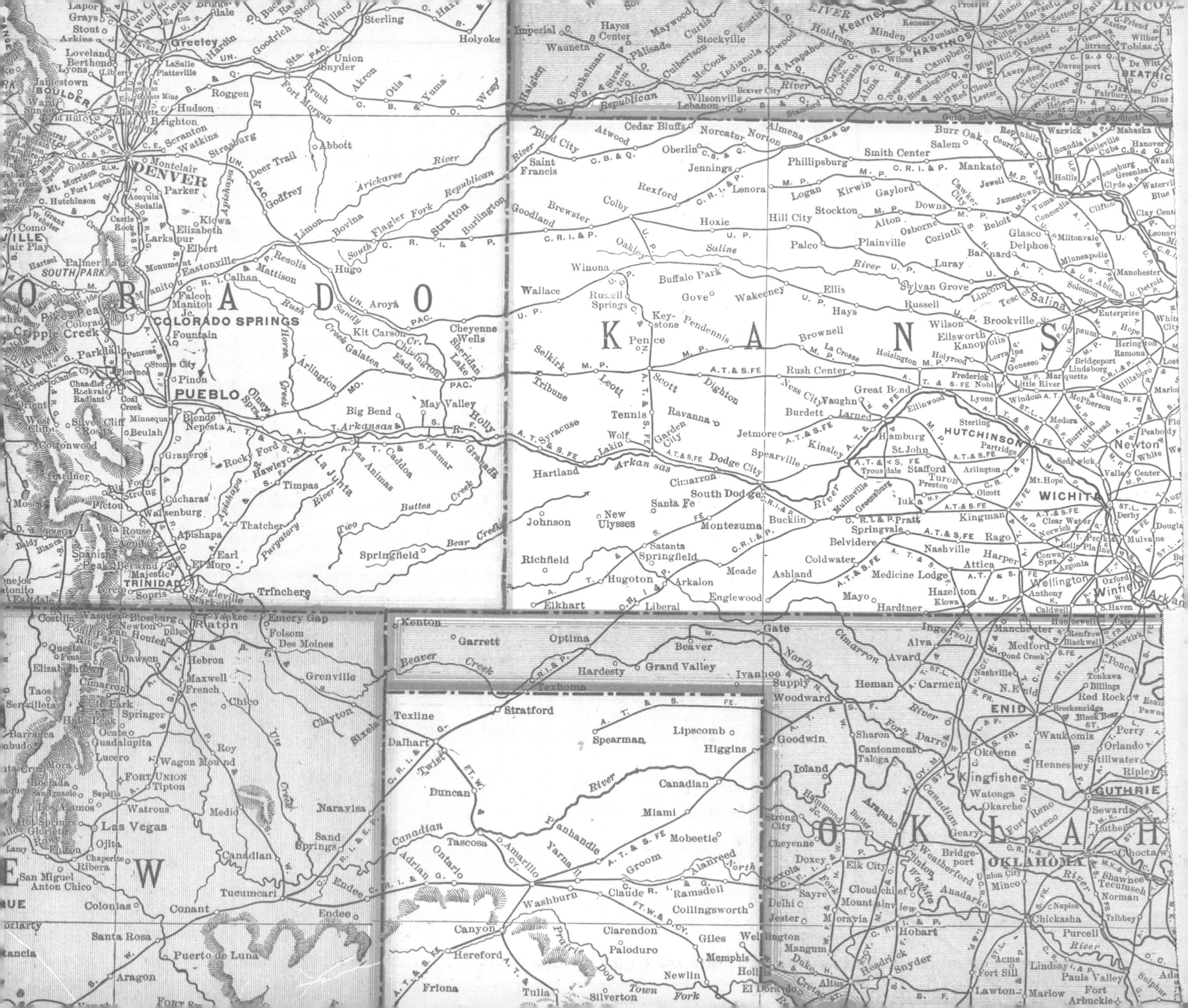

DENVER
Greeley
Boulder
Sterling
Holyoke
Fort Morgan
Brush
Akron
Yuma
Wray
Limon
Hugo
COLORADO SPRINGS
Pikes Peak
Cripple Creek
PUEBLO
Trinidad
Walsenburg
La Junta
Rocky Ford
Las Animas
Lamar
Holly
Granada
Springfield
Cheyenne Wells
Kit Carson
Eads
Arkansas
Purgatory River
Republican
Arickaree
O R A D O
Imperial
McCook
Holdrege
Kearney
Minden
HASTINGS
Beatrice
Republican River
Saint Francis
Bird City
Atwood
Oberlin
Norton
Phillipsburg
Smith Center
Mankato
Colby
Goodland
Hill City
Stockton
Beloit
Concordia
Wallace
Oakley
Wakeeney
Hays
Russell
Ellis
Salina
Abilene
Ellsworth
K A N S
Scott
Dighton
Ness City
Great Bend
Larned
Garden City
Dodge City
Kinsley
Spearville
HUTCHINSON
Newton
Sterling
McPherson
WICHITA
Kingman
Pratt
Medicine Lodge
Wellington
Winfield
Arkansas
Hugoton
Liberal
Meade
Ashland
Coldwater
Elkhart
Richfield
Johnson
Raton
Cimarron
Springer
Clayton
Las Vegas
Tucumcari
Santa Rosa
Puerto de Luna
Fort Union
Wagon Mound
Kenton
Beaver
Texhoma
Texline
Dalhart
Stratford
Spearman
Lipscomb
Higgins
Canadian
Miami
Mobeetie
Panhandle
Amarillo
Tascosa
Canyon
Hereford
Tulia
Clarendon
Memphis
Wellington
Canadian River
Woodward
Alva
Enid
Kingfisher
GUTHRIE
Stillwater
Perry
OKLAHOMA
El Reno
Chickasha
Anadarko
Lawton
Fort Sill
Hobart
Mangum
Altus
O K L A H